ATLAS OF EXPLORATION

Authors

Anita Ganeri
Andrea Mills

Consultant

Anne Millard

D1136816

DK

LONDON, NEW YORK,
MELBOURNE, MUNICH, AND DELHI

Senior art editor Philip Letsu
Senior editor Shaila Brown
Project art editors Marilou Prokopiou, Sheila Collins
Project editors Fran Jones, Andrea Mills, Jenny Finch
Managing editor Linda Esposito
Managing art editor Diane Thistlethwaite
Publishing manager Andrew Macintyre
Category publisher Laura Buller
Picture researcher Frances Vargo
DK picture library Rose Horridge, Emma Shepherd
Production controller Angela Graef
Production editor Andy Hilliard
Jacket editor Mariza O'Keeffe
Jacket designer Natasha Rees
Jacket manager Sophia M Tampakopoulos Turner
Cartographer Ed Merritt
Illustrator Andrew Kerr
CD-Rom developers Andrew Kerr, François Naudé
CD-Rom project manager Anthony Pearson

First published in Great Britain in 2008 by
Dorling Kindersley Limited, 80 Strand, London WC2R 0RL

2 4 6 8 10 9 7 5 3 1

Copyright © 2008 Dorling Kindersley Limited, London
A Penguin Company

ISBN: 978-1-40532-208-9

Colour reproduction by Colourscan, Singapore
Printed and bound in Honk Kong

Discover more at
www.dk.com

How to run Atlas of Exploration CD-ROM
Please note that this multimedia program will run best if you
close any other applications that you may have open.

Windows® PC
Insert the disk into your computer's CD-ROM drive.
The CD-Rom will launch automatically.

Apple Macintosh®
Insert the disk into your computer's CD-ROM drive. Double click
on the Atlas of Exploration CD-ROM icon to open the CD window.

Minimum system requirements
Windows® PC
Intel Pentium® 4 2.4 GHz or higher recommended
Windows® 98SE, 2000, XP (Vista compliance not guaranteed)
256Mb RAM or higher recommended
32-bit colour monitor capable of 1024 x 768 resolution
Hardware accelerated 3D graphics card with 16Mb or more of VRAM
DirectX 7.0 or higher recommended
32x speed CD-ROM drive
Windows compatible sound card

Apple Macintosh®
PowerPC G5 1.6 GHz or higher recommended
Mac® OSX 10.2 or higher recommended
256Mb RAM or higher recommended
32-bit colour monitor capable of 1024 x 768 resolution
Hardware accelerated 3D graphics card with 16Mb or more of VRAM
Open GL 1.1.2 or higher recommended
32x speed CD-ROM drive

Contents

Early Explorers

FROM THE BEGINNING of human history people have explored their surroundings and ventured into unknown lands. In the remote past, people covered great distances in search of the animals they hunted for food. These early journeys were governed by the seasons and the migration of the animals. It was with the development of the earliest civilizations that planned exploration really began and some explorers left records of their journeys. Even with limited means of transport, early explorers, traders, and colonists were prepared to undertake dangerous journeys of months – even years – to obtain the goods or lands they desired.

6–7 TRAVELLING TRADERS

The first great voyages of exploration took place around the Middle East. Seafarers set sail for new lands, largely driven by the need to trade. Among these early explorers were the Egyptians, Mesopotamians, Minoans, and Mycenaeans.

Ancient Egyptian relief shows soldiers preparing for Punt.

8–9 PURPLE MEN

By about 1000 BC, the Canaanites and later the Phoenicians had become the greatest traders in the Mediterranean. The Phoenicians were also known as the "Purple Men", because of their most valuable export – purple dye.

The murex shellfish was the source of the precious purple dye.

10–11 ANCIENT POLYNESIANS

From c. 2000 BC, Polynesians from southeast Asia set sail across the vast Pacific Ocean.

These stone statues on Easter Island were carved by the Polynesians who settled there.

12–13 CARTHAGINIANS

In c. 500 BC, Hanno sailed around the west coast of Africa, while Himilco headed towards Europe.

Hippopotamuses in an African river.

14–15 GREEK ADVENTURES

With the founding of colonies around the Mediterranean, the Greek world expanded. Greek merchants, explorers, and soldiers also made daring journeys, reaching as far as the Indus River (in modern Pakistan).

Gemstones were brought back from India by Greek explorers.

16–17 CHINESE TRAVELLERS

Two thousand years ago, merchants carried costly silks from China to Europe along a series of trade routes called the Silk Road. Religious and artistic ideas were also exchanged between East and West.

The ruins of a caravanserai (rest house) along the Silk Road.

18–19 ROMAN EXPLORATION

Exploration was largely concerned with expanding the Roman Empire and conquering new lands and peoples. But Roman exploration was also influenced by Greek geographers living under Roman rule and by the desire for luxury goods from the East.

This 15th-century-AD world map was based on a work by Ptolemy, a Greek geographer living in Roman Egypt during AD 100.

20–21 ARAB TRAVELLERS

From the 9th century AD onwards, Arab travellers made long journeys into Africa and the Far East, while Arabs scholars made discoveries in geography and astronomy.

The compass was used by Muslims to help find the direction of Mecca.

22–23 VIKING VOYAGES

From around AD 800, the Vikings from Scandinavia made extraordinary voyages across the Atlantic Ocean, Europe, and Asia.

The Vikings used ships like this, called a knorr, for transporting cargo.

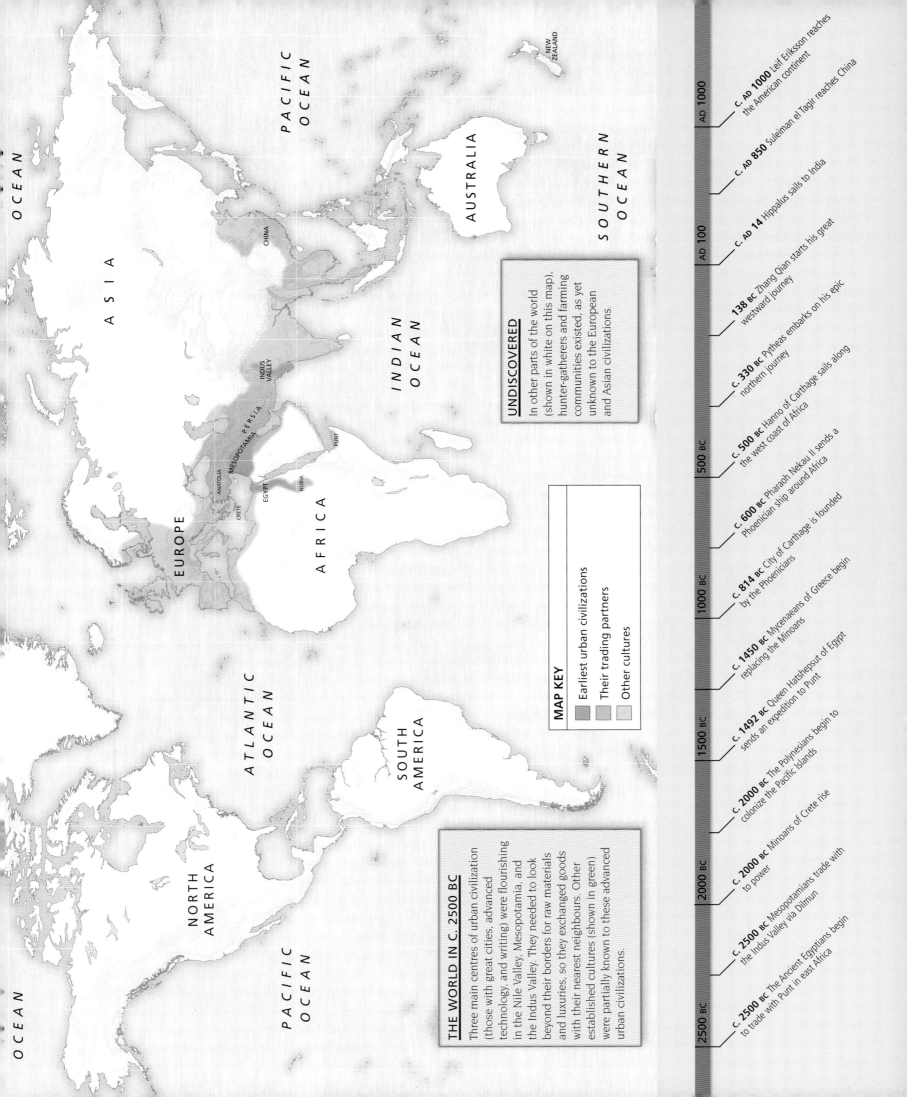

OCEAN

OCEAN

PACIFIC
OCEAN

NEW
ZEALAND

ASIA

A S I A

EUROPE

CHINA

INDUS
VALLEY

PERSIA

ANATOLIA

MESOPOTAMIA

CRETE

EGYPT

PUNT

NUBIA

AFRICA

INDIAN
OCEAN

AUSTRALIA

SOUTHERN
OCEAN

NORTH
AMERICA

ATLANTIC
OCEAN

SOUTH
AMERICA

PACIFIC
OCEAN

THE WORLD IN C. 2500 BC

Three main centres of urban civilization (those with great cities, advanced technology, and writing) were flourishing in the Nile Valley, Mesopotamia, and the Indus Valley. They needed to look beyond their borders for raw materials and luxuries, so they exchanged goods with their nearest neighbours. Other established cultures (shown in green) were partially known to these advanced urban civilizations.

MAP KEY

- Earliest urban civilizations
- Their trading partners
- Other cultures

UNDISCOVERED

In other parts of the world (shown in white on this map), hunter-gatherers and farming communities existed, as yet unknown to the European and Asian civilizations.

AD 1000

AD 100

500 BC

1000 BC

1500 BC

2000 BC

2500 BC

c. AD 1000 Leif Eriksson reaches the American continent

c. AD 850 Suleiman el Tagir reaches China

c. AD 14 Hippalus sails to India

138 BC Zhang Qian starts his great westward journey

c. 330 BC Pytheas embarks on his epic northern journey

c. 500 BC Hanno of Carthage sails along the west coast of Africa

c. 600 BC Pharaoh Nekau II sends a Phoenician ship around Africa

c. 814 BC City of Carthage is founded by the Phoenicians

c. 1450 BC Mycenaeans of Greece begin replacing the Minoans

c. 1492 BC Queen Hatshepsut of Egypt sends an expedition to Punt

c. 2000 BC The Polynesians begin to colonize the Pacific Islands

c. 2000 BC Minoans of Crete rise to power

c. 2500 BC Mesopotamians trade with the Indus Valley via Dilmun

c. 2500 BC The Ancient Egyptians begin to trade with Punt in east Africa

Travelling Traders

THE EARLIEST GREAT CIVILIZATIONS – Egypt, Mesopotamia, and the Indus Valley – evolved in the fertile river valleys of the Nile, the Tigris and Euphrates, and the Indus. They built cities and invented forms of writing. The wealth of these civilizations was based on farming but, from their very beginnings, the Egyptians and Mesopotamians were also traders. Merchants ranged far and wide, by land and sea, seeking out not only raw materials such as timber from Byblos, but also foreign luxury goods. The same impulse drove the Minoans of Crete and the Mycenaean Greeks.

MAP KEY

⊥—	Egyptian trade routes
◄—	Mesopotamian trade routes
◄—	Minoan trade routes
◄—	Mycenaean trade routes

◄ HARKHUF

The Egyptian nobleman Harkhuf, who lived around 2300 BC, is the first well-documented explorer. In his tomb at Aswân, Egypt, he records his expeditions into Nubia and tells of how he was involved in a war between the tribes there, which threatened his trade routes. On his journeys, he travelled overland, taking with him caravans of donkeys 300 strong.

EGYPTIAN SOLDIERS rejoicing that Queen Hatshepsut will send them to Punt

INCENSE SEEKERS ►

About 2500 BC, the Egyptians made an incredible journey to the land of Punt – thought to be the Horn of Africa and the source of highly prized frankincense and myrrh. From the Nile Valley, boats were carried in pieces across the Eastern Desert and reassembled on the Red Sea coast. Soon expeditions were regularly making the dangerous journey to Punt. In c. 1492 BC, after a long interruption, Queen Hatshepsut sent out another expedition to restart the trade. Besides incense, the expedition brought back goods such as gold, ivory, and ebony.

WALL PAINTING FOUND ON THE ISLAND
OF THERA SHOWING A CRETAN SHIP

MINOAN MARINERS ▲

From about 2000 BC, the Minoans of Crete rose to power and became leading players in the world of Mediterranean trade, exporting goods such as wine, oil, and jewellery in return for raw materials and food. They set up trading posts along the coast of Asia Minor (modern Turkey) and, under the direction of their rulers, carried and traded goods for other people. This trade made the Minoans fabulously wealthy.

MESOPOTAMIAN TRAVELS ▶

The wealthy city-states of early Mesopotamia (modern Iraq) were enthusiastic traders. Their caravans journeyed west to Byblos on the Mediterranean coast, while Mesopotamian sailors explored the Persian Gulf and traded with the people of the Indus Valley. The island of Dilmun (modern Bahrain) became an important staging post where merchants of Mesopotamia and the Indus Valley could meet and trade.

STONE SEALS USED BY
INDUS VALLEY MERCHANTS
TO SEAL BUNDLES OF GOODS

STONE RELIEF SHOWING JASON
TAKING THE GOLDEN FLEECE

GOLD RING
DEPICTING A
MYCENAEAN SHIP

▲ MYCENAEANS

By about 1450 BC, the decline in Minoan power allowed the Mycenaeans to take over both the trade and trading posts of the Minoans. The Mycenaeans also appear to have been explorers, venturing into the then unknown lands along the Black Sea.

THE GOLDEN FLEECE ▲

One Greek legend tells of how Jason and his men set sail on the *Argo* to distant Colchis (modern Georgia) and stole the fabulous Golden Fleece. The tale was probably based on Mycenaean voyages of exploration made to the gold-rich land of Colchis.

Purple Men

FOR MANY CENTURIES, the Canaanites and later their descendants the Phoenicians dominated trade in the Mediterranean and the Middle East. They were some of the greatest traders, sailors, and explorers of the ancient world. Their great ports along the eastern Mediterranean coasts became centres of commercial power, the greatest being Byblos, Tyre, and Sidon (in modern Lebanon). They also established trading colonies around the French, Spanish, and African coasts. Their homeland had two precious commodities that were sought by their powerful neighbours – cedar wood and purple dye. This important trade in purple dye led to the Greeks calling them Phoenicians ("Purple Men").

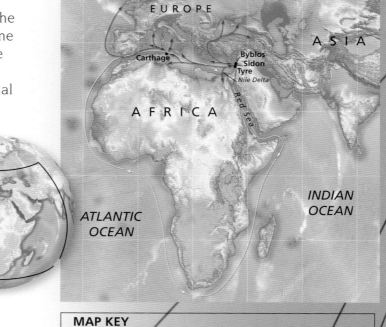

MAP KEY

← Canaanite and Phoenician trade routes
↙ Nekau II's expedition (c. 600 BC)

TRADING SHIP ▶

This reconstruction of a trading ship used by the Canaanites and the Phoenicians was based on wrecks discovered by marine archaeologists. Such ships sailed the Mediterranean and beyond, buying, selling, and setting up depots. The greatest powers of the day – Egypt, Mesopotamia, and the Hittite lands (modern Turkey) – were their best customers.

CROSS-SECTION ▶

The trading ship was broad and strong, and made from the best cedar wood. The ship was painted with tar to help make it watertight. A single square sail was used to power the ship, while two huge oars were used for guiding it. The cargo, which was kept below deck, was stored in pottery jars and secured with ropes.

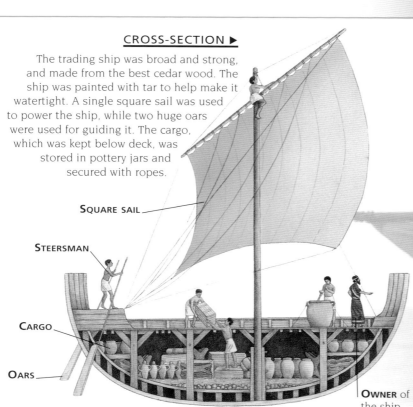
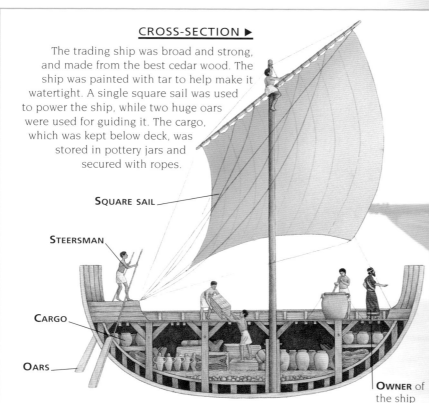

SQUARE SAIL

STEERSMAN

CARGO

OARS

OWNER of the ship

◄ NAVIGATION

The Canaanites and the Phoenicians were highly skilled sailors, venturing into unknown lands in search of trade. Like all ancient sailors, they tended to sail within sight of the coast, navigating by known landmarks. They tried to avoid sailing in winter, but took advantage of seasonal winds. They also learned to observe the sky and, at night, were guided by the Pole Star.

CARVING OF
TRADING SHIP
shows just how
important trade
was to the
Phoenicians

DETAIL FROM STONE COFFIN

TRADE ►

Many goods were traded, such as glass, cedar oil, and timber. In return, the Phoenicians bought raw materials, such as copper and gold, which they then sold to neighbouring peoples. One of their key exports, however, was purple dye. It was so expensive that only the very rich could afford it. The purple dye came from the murex shellfish. Extracting the dye was a long and costly business.

MUREX SHELLFISH

◄ EXPLORING AFRICA

So great was their reputation as fearless, adventurous sailors, that when Egypt's Pharaoh Nekau II wanted to send an expedition to explore Africa in 600 BC, he employed Phoenician sailors. The astonishing journey around the entire coast of Africa — a distance of 25,000 km (15,500 miles) – is said to have taken three years.

ENGRAVING SHOWING PHARAOH
NEKAU INSTRUCTING THE FLEET

Pharaoh Nekau II

From 610–595 BC, Egypt was ruled by Pharaoh Nekau II. He was an enterprising and imaginative ruler. He won victories against the newly expanded Babylonian Empire, and had great plans for trade and travel. One of his plans was to dig a canal between the River Nile and the Red Sea to make trade between east and west quicker and easier. The project, however, was never completed.

Ancient Polynesians

SOME OF THE MOST REMARKABLE, epic journeys in the history of exploration were made by the Polynesians. From about 2000 BC, they set sail from southeast Asia, crossing the Pacific – the world's largest ocean. Scattered across it are thousands of islands, and with only their knowledge of nature to guide them, the Polynesians discovered most of them. As the population grew on one group of islands, they set out to find uninhabited islands. This long process of exploration continued until one group, the Maoris, reached New Zealand in about AD 1000.

Hawaiian Islands
Marshall Islands
Line Islands
Galapagos Islands
New Guinea
Solomon Islands
Tuvalu
Samoa
Marquesas Islands
Vanuatu
New Caledonia
Fiji
Tonga
Society Islands
Easter Island
New Zealand

MAP KEY

Routes taken by the Polynesians

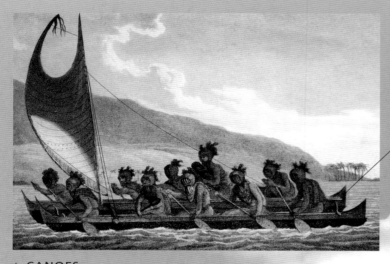

CANOES were powered along by triangular sails as well as paddles

STATUES were up to 20 m (65 ft) tall and weighed up to 45 tonnes (44 tons)

▲ CANOES

The Polynesians made their extraordinary voyages in dug-out canoes. The ocean-going versions had two hulls joined together by a central platform that had a cabin and mast. Some canoes were large enough to carry people, animals, water, and food supplies. Conditions on board would have been difficult for settlers travelling such vast distances with their animals and plants.

TOPKNOTS (crowns) carved from a dark red stone came from a different quarry than the stone used for the bodies

ISLAND NAVIGATION ▶

The Polynesians were naturally skilled sailors. Armed with their knowledge of cloud formations, the stars, wave patterns, and migrating birds, they were able to find their way across the vast ocean. They also made maps from twigs tied together – the twigs represented an area of sea, while shells attached to the framework represented islands. Such a map enabled the sailors to return home and make the journey again, taking with them their families and possessions.

FRAMEWORK OF STICKS represented thousands of kilometres of ocean

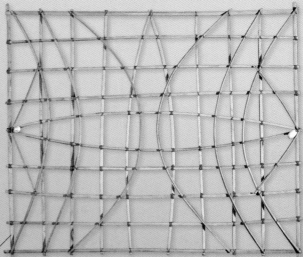

◀ MAORIS

One group of Polynesians, the Maoris, began to arrive in New Zealand from about AD 1000. They developed their own distinct culture. They lived in small tribes ruled by a chief. The Maoris who lived on North Island were mostly farmers, while those of the South Island lived by fishing, gathering plants, and hunting birds and sea mammals.

MODERN-DAY MAORI wearing traditional dress and decorated with tattoos

◀ EASTER ISLAND STATUES

The most isolated of all the Polynesian islands is Easter Island. No wider than 38 km (24 miles), and more than 1,600 km (900 miles) from its neighbouring island, Easter Island was settled by the Polynesians who developed their own form of writing and built gigantic stone statues.

DID YOU KNOW?

▶ Archaeologists have been able to trace the movements of one group of Polynesians from the pottery they made. Broken pieces of this patterned pottery, called Lapita ware, together with tools have been found on various Pacific Islands.

Carthaginians

In about 814 BC, Phoenician colonists founded a city on the north coast of Africa and called it Carthage ("New City"). Thanks to its prime location, Carthage quickly grew in size and stature to become the Mediterranean's maritime powerhouse. Its citizens prospered as wealthy shipping traders, setting up highly successful colonies in places such as Spain, Sicily, and Sardinia. These intrepid explorers travelled widely in search of new sources of raw materials, especially metals and the famous purple dye of the time. The city's most celebrated adventurers were Hanno, a leading politician, and Himilco, a local sailor. As Hanno took his fleet south to the west coast of Africa, Himilco ventured north to unknown areas of Europe.

▼ CARTHAGE HARBOUR

Among the most impressive of Carthage's many magnificent buildings was the harbour and dockyard, shown in this reconstruction. The harbour sheltered trading vessels and Carthage's fleet of warships. The inner circular dockyard had extensive facilities for building and repairing ships. Like the rest of Carthage, it was totally destroyed by the Romans at the end of three bloody wars fought between 264 BC and 146 BC.

MAP KEY
- ⟿ Stage 1 of Hanno's voyage (c. 500 BC)
- ⬅ Stage 2 of Hanno's voyage (c. 500 BC)
- ⬅ Himilco's voyage (c. 500 BC)

HANNO'S MISSION ▶

With a fleet of 60 large ships loaded with colonists, Hanno sailed through the Pillars of Hercules (Strait of Gibraltar), the passage linking the Mediterranean Sea to the Atlantic Ocean. He set up seven colonies along the African coastline to guard the route to Madeira and the Canary Islands, two locations where fresh sources of dye had been found.

VOLCANIC ERUPTION ▼

The lure of exploration sometimes led Hanno's fleet into unexpected dangers. On the voyage south, the men witnessed a volcano erupting. Flames shot into the sky and molten lava poured down the mountain, so the Earth appeared to be on fire. The volcano was either Mount Cameroon or Mount Kakulima. It is still uncertain how far Hanno's expedition travelled – modern Sierra Leone, Cameroon, and Gabon are all possibilities.

◀ AMAZING ANIMALS

Instead of returning home after setting up the colonies, Hanno headed further south. He saw extraordinary animals, including hippopotamuses and crocodiles at the mouth of the River Senegal. On one island, he reported seeing troops of hairy people, but these were probably chimpanzees.

MOUNT CAMEROON remains an active volcano, and is seen here erupting in 1999

TRAVEL RECORD ▶

Hanno had to turn back when his provisions started running out. On his return, he is said to have set up an inscription recording his epic voyage in the temple of the god Ba'al Hammon in Carthage. The inscription was translated in this Greek manuscript called the *Periplus*.

▲ TIN ISLANDS

About the time of Hanno's voyage, Himilco set sail from the port of Marseille in search of the Tin Islands, said to be in the north Atlantic. He reached Brittany, the centre of the northern tin trade, and he may also have sailed to Cornwall and the Isles of Scilly, shown here. As a result, Carthage monopolized the northern tin trade.

DID YOU KNOW?

▶ The Romans lacked proper warships in their first two wars with Carthage. Upon seizing a Carthaginian war galley, they copied it and built a fleet. These ships helped the Romans overcome Carthage in 146 BC.

Greek Adventures

OUT OF THE ASHES of the Mycenaean trading empire a new Greek culture emerged and thrived from about 800 BC onwards. As the Greeks prospered, the population grew and many Greeks ventured into other areas. They set up colonies in Italy, along the Black Sea, and as far as North Africa. These colonies provided vital trading partners and depots for Greek merchants. Some Greek explorers also set out in search of new lands because they wanted to learn more about the world. But under the leadership of one of history's greatest military leaders, Alexander the Great, a new reason was found for exploration – that of conquest.

MAP KEY

→ Route of Alexander the Great (334–323 BC)
→ Voyage of Pytheas (c. 330–320 BC)
→ Eudoxus's outward journey (c. 146 BC)
→ Eudoxus's return journey (c. 146 BC)

▶ ALEXANDER'S TRAVELS

In 331 BC, Alexander the Great conquered the mighty Persian Empire, then marched east through the dangerous Hindu Kush. After a gruelling 32,000 km (20,000 miles), he reached the Indus in 326 BC before turning back. The conquests of Alexander opened up new horizons for the Greeks. Within a decade, he had conquered an empire that stretched across three continents, creating a vast network for trade.

HINDU KUSH MOUNTAIN RANGE

▶ NORTHERN EUROPE

In about 330 BC, Greek geographer and astronomer Pytheas set sail from Massalia (modern-day Marseille) to explore northern Europe. He became the first explorer that we know of to sail around the British Isles, and the first to give an account of the people who lived there. He also visited a place called Thule, which modern research suggests was Iceland.

RUBY

EMERALD

SAPPHIRE

PEARLS

▶ PRICELESS CARGO

One of the most daring ancient voyages was made by Greek explorer Eudoxus of Cyzicus. Around 146 BC, he was instructed by the Egyptian pharaoh Ptolemy VIII to sail to India. His guide, an Indian sailor, revealed to him the secret of the monsoon winds, giving him quicker journeys to and from India. Eudoxus returned with a priceless cargo of spices and gemstones.

SHETLAND ISLANDS would have been seen by Pytheas on his journey

Alexander the Great

Born in the Greek kingdom of Macedonia, Alexander the Great (356–323 BC) was a fearless and gifted general. He became King of Macedonia when he was only 20 years old, and led his army into lands previously unknown to the Greeks.

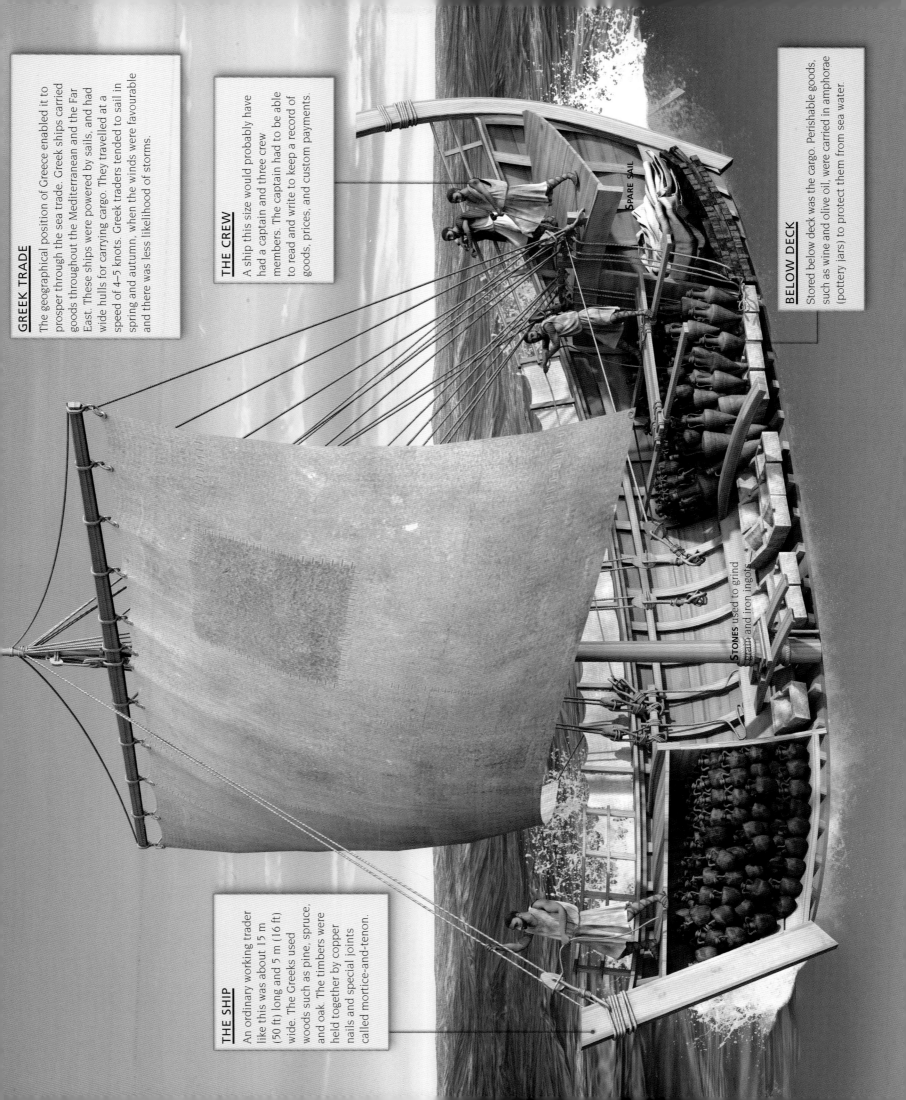

GREEK TRADE

The geographical position of Greece enabled it to prosper through the sea trade. Greek ships carried goods throughout the Mediterranean and the Far East. These ships were powered by sails, and had wide hulls for carrying cargo. They travelled at a speed of 4–5 knots. Greek traders tended to sail in spring and autumn, when the winds were favourable and there was less likelihood of storms.

THE CREW

A ship this size would probably have had a captain and three crew members. The captain had to be able to read and write to keep a record of goods, prices, and custom payments.

BELOW DECK

Stored below deck was the cargo. Perishable goods, such as wine and olive oil, were carried in amphorae (pottery jars) to protect them from sea water.

THE SHIP

An ordinary working trader like this was about 15 m (50 ft) long and 5 m (16 ft) wide. The Greeks used woods such as pine, spruce, and oak. The timbers were held together by copper nails and special joints called mortice-and-tenon.

SPARE SAIL

STONES used to grind grain and iron ingots

Chinese Travellers

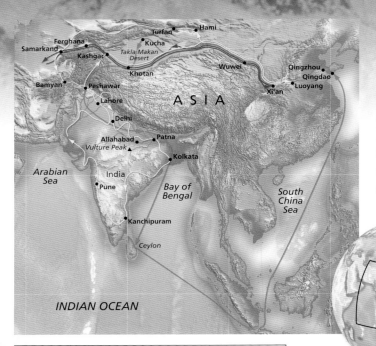

INDIAN OCEAN

MAP KEY

- Zhang Qian's route (138–116 BC)
- Faxian's route (AD 399–414)
- Xuangzang's route (AD 629–645)

FOR THE FIRST TIME IN ITS HISTORY, China became a united nation in the year 221 BC. Rival states were unified by Emperor Shihuangdi, and the country's turbulent period of war and instability ended. The only threat now facing the civilization came from a violent group of nomadic tribesmen called the Huns. The search for allies to support China against the Huns, coupled with the desire to find the best breeds of horses, resulted in the opening of the world's most famous trade route – the Silk Road. This challenging path started in China and ran 4,000 km (2,500 miles) across central Asia's mountains, deserts, and plains to the shores of the Mediterranean. As the name suggests, silk was the main commodity sent west by the Chinese. In return, they received gold, silver, pearls, glass, and horses. But the route was not just a means of exchanging goods. The Silk Road became integral to the spread of religions, cultures, and ideas between East and West.

◀ HEAVENLY HORSES

In 138 BC, the emperor's official, Zhang Qian, travelled west to find allies prepared to fight against China's enemies, the Huns. His mission failed and he was held prisoner by the Huns for a decade. Despite this, he learned of the existence of the Roman Empire, and in Ferghana saw the "heavenly" or "flying" horses, that were much faster and stronger than Chinese breeds.

BRONZE STATUE OF A "FLYING" HORSE FROM ABOUT AD 200

▼ REST STOPS

In China, goods were loaded on to camels and the traders set off on the long, slow journey west. Travelling along any branch of the Silk Road was difficult and dangerous. Besides the hazardous landscape, there were bandits and wild animals to contend with. To ease the journey, special rest houses called caravanserais were built along the way. They provided safe and comfortable stopping points for weary merchants and their animals. Shown here is the Tash Rabat caravanserai. It is the only completely preserved rest house on the old Silk Road.

DID YOU KNOW?

As long ago as 2700 BC, the Chinese learned how to make silk from the cocoons of silkworm moths. They kept it a government secret for about 3,000 years. Silk was so important to the Chinese economy that anyone revealing the secret of silk-making was sentenced to death.

CHINESE ENGRAVING
OF XUANGZANG

▲ THE RISE OF BUDDHISM

This huge statue of the Buddha used to stand in Bamyan (in modern Afghanistan). The religion of Buddhism began in India in the 6th century BC and quickly spread through much of Asia. It reached China via the Silk Road in about AD 100. During the centuries that followed, Chinese Buddhist monks became intrepid explorers, making daring journeys along the Silk Road to India to learn more about their religion.

▲ INDIAN EXPERIENCE

The Chinese Buddhist monk Faxian set off for India in AD 399, travelling across the perilous Takla Makan Desert. From there, he passed mountains said to shelter dragons, before reaching his destination. He spent 15 years in India, visiting sacred sites, such as Vulture Peak, where the Buddha taught his followers.

▲ RELIGIOUS TREASURES

Two hundred years later, another monk, Xuangzang, followed in Faxian's footsteps. When he returned to China in AD 645, he brought back more than 700 religious manuscripts, together with statues of the Buddha and other artefacts. He spent the rest of his life teaching Buddhism and writing a book of his travels.

Roman Exploration

FOR THE ANCIENT ROMANS, it was conquest rather than curiosity that led them to explore new and distant lands. Constantly trying to expand the frontiers of the mighty Roman Empire, their soldiers marched across North Africa, the Middle East, and Europe. Each region was meticulously mapped and measured, adding to an enormous fund of geographical information. This information helped the Romans to build up a detailed picture of the world they wished to rule.

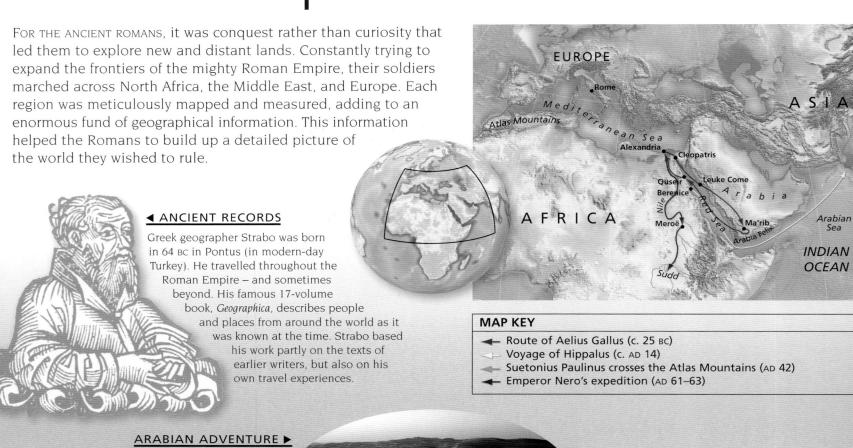

◄ ANCIENT RECORDS

Greek geographer Strabo was born in 64 BC in Pontus (in modern-day Turkey). He travelled throughout the Roman Empire – and sometimes beyond. His famous 17-volume book, *Geographica*, describes people and places from around the world as it was known at the time. Strabo based his work partly on the texts of earlier writers, but also on his own travel experiences.

MAP KEY

◄— Route of Aelius Gallus (c. 25 BC)
◁— Voyage of Hippalus (c. AD 14)
◄— Suetonius Paulinus crosses the Atlas Mountains (AD 42)
◄— Emperor Nero's expedition (AD 61–63)

ARABIAN ADVENTURE ►

In 25 BC, Emperor Augustus sent Aelius Gallus to explore Arabia – a source of valuable incense. Despite the heat, Gallus and his army made progress along the fertile coastal regions. When they reached the deserts, however, it was a different story. Six months later, many were dead from heat and thirst. The survivors staggered home with nothing to show for their travels.

TOWERING SAND DUNES, lack of water, and the extreme, dry heat proved to be insurmountable obstacles

ARABIAN DESERT

NERO AND THE NILE ▶

In AD 61, Emperor Nero sent an expedition south to search for the source of the River Nile. On the way, the soldiers visited the wealthy African kingdom of Meroë before their journey was blocked by a huge, muddy marsh. This was the Sudd, a vast papyrus swamp (near the border with modern Uganda).

◢ EXOTIC IMPORTS

Rich Roman citizens, and later Byzantines (like Empress Theodora above), dressed in silks from China. Romans also craved other Eastern luxuries, so traders undertook ever more daring sea voyages. In AD 14, Hippalus sailed from the Red Sea to India, taking advantage of the monsoon winds. From then on, traders used the "Hippalus winds", as they called them, to sail to India.

◢ THE ATLAS MOUNTAINS

In AD 42, Suetonius Paulinus was sent to quell an uprising in northern Morocco. When some of the rebels fled, he set off in pursuit and, by chance, became the first European to explore and cross the great Atlas Mountains.

◀ PTOLEMY'S WORLD VIEW

In about AD 150, Ptolemy, a Greek astronomer working in Roman Egypt, produced a guide to mapping the known world. His eight-volume *Geographia* contained instructions on map-making and a list of 8,000 places, together with tables of latitude and longitude. Ptolemy's work survived and so had great influence on future generations of explorers.

MAP OF THE WORLD dates from 1482, but is based on Ptolemy's *Geographia*

DID YOU KNOW?

The most expensive of perfumes imported by Ancient Rome was malabathron. It was made from the leaves of the cinnamon plant, which originally came from Ceylon (Sri Lanka). Rome's merchants bought other luxuries from India such as pearls, jewels, and even tigers.

Arab Travellers

THE ISLAMIC FAITH began in the 7th century in Arabia (modern Saudi Arabia). Two hundred years later, Islam had spread across a vast area, stretching from Spain to India. The followers of Islam, called Muslims, were great explorers and scholars. They travelled far and wide, spreading their faith, culture, and learning, and collecting a wealth of geographical information. This was used to guide Arab merchants who traded in Africa, India, and China, and Muslim pilgrims who were making the long and difficult journey to the holy city of Mecca.

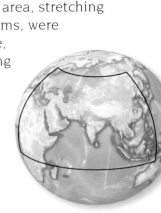

EARLY COMPASS
invented by the Chinese
was used by the Arabs

MAP KEY

⟵ Suleiman el Tagir's voyage (c. AD 850)
⟵ Ibn Fadlan's route (AD 921–922)

◀ RIGHT DIRECTION

The Arabs were skilled geographers and scientists. They considered geography to be a combination of three sciences – geology, astronomy, and astrology. Ancient navigational tools that depended on the position of the Sun and stars were used by Arabs to guide them on journeys of exploration, trade, or pilgrimage. The compass was useful for pilgrims because it established the position of Mecca, towards which daily prayers were addressed. It also helped to guide pilgrims to the holy city.

DID YOU KNOW?

In 1324 the wealthy King of Mali, Mansa Musa, went on a pilgrimage to Mecca. He and his group of 60,000 stopped at Cairo on the way. He paid for everything in gold and spent so much that the value of the local money collapsed. It took 12 years to recover.

CHIEFTAIN'S SHIP was laden down with provisons

OLD WOMAN called the "angel of death" was responsible for killing the sacrificial slave girl

THE MERCHANT

One of the great trading adventurers was Suleiman el Tagir, known as "The Merchant". A citizen of Siraf on the Persian Gulf, el Tagir set off on an epic voyage to India and China in AD 850. He sailed across the Indian Ocean to Kerala (shown here) in southern India. From there, he continued to Singapore and on to Canton. Later, he wrote a book of his experiences.

THE OBSERVERS

Some Arab travellers wrote fascinating accounts of their experiences. In AD 921, Arab adventurer Ibn Fadlan was sent on a religious mission to the Bolgars, who were new converts to Islam. While travelling along the River Volga, he met a group of Vikings, called the Rus. Ibn Fadlan saw their chieftain's funeral and later wrote about it.

◀ SCHOLARS

Abu Rayhan al-Biruni was one of the greatest of the many Arab scholars. He produced books on astronomy, geology, mathematics, and geography. Such books contributed to Arab explorers' knowledge of the world.

◀ THE SAILOR

The famous story of Sinbad the sailor was partly based on the experiences of Arab explorers who sailed around the Indian Ocean. The story tells of a merchant, Sinbad, who went on seven adventure-filled voyages to distant lands. Sinbad is shown in this engraving from an 1895 edition of the book.

TORCH was used to set the ship ablaze

LAID TO REST

The chieftain's body was laid out on his ship. All his worldly goods, including his prized weapons, were placed beside his body. A slave girl was sacrificed and put next to the chieftain to join him on his journey to the next world.

ANIMALS, including a horse, a dog, and a chicken, were killed as sacrifices and stored in the ship

IBN FADLAN was shocked by the funeral ritual

Viking Voyages

IN THE LATE 8TH CENTURY, the people of Scandinavia were driven to seek their fortunes abroad in a series of remarkable voyages. They had prospered in their homelands of Denmark, Norway, and Sweden, working as farmers, craftspeople, and merchants. The population, however, had grown, and the limited farmland could no longer support them all. So, some set off in search of treasure and new homes, taking both by force from existing settlements if necessary. Called the Vikings, they quickly gained a reputation as ruthless raiders, terrorizing western Europe and beyond.

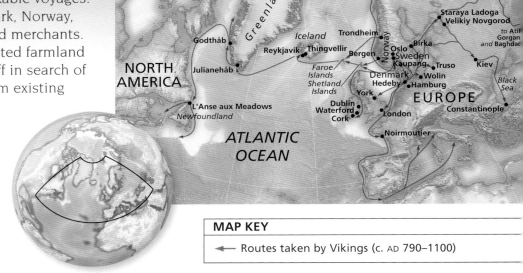

MAP KEY

← Routes taken by Vikings (c. AD 790–1100)

▲ TRADING EASTWARDS

Some Viking traders sailed east along the rivers in what became Russia. When travelling by river, Vikings used small, light boats, such as the one in this woodcut. For travelling across open seas or transporting colonists to new homes, they sailed in a large vessel known as a knorr. A large knorr could carry 40 people, together with cattle and food.

KNORRS carried Vikings long distances to new settlements

◄ FAR AND WIDE

The Vikings' voyages took them west across the Atlantic Ocean to Iceland, Greenland, and North America, and east through Russia into Asia. While some Swedish Vikings established trade routes as far as the Black Sea and Caspian Sea, many Norwegian Vikings settled in Scotland and Ireland. Danish Vikings were busy colonizing England and raiding the coastlines of North Africa, Spain, and Italy.

VIKING CUSTOMS ▶

After establishing homes in the Shetland and Faroe Islands during the early AD 800s, some Vikings braved stormy seas to reach Iceland. After settling in, the Vikings flourished. They took their way of life, customs, and gods with them, including Thor, god of thunder, who the Vikings believed used his great hammer to protect the gods from the giants.

BRONZE STATUE OF THOR FROM ABOUT AD 1000

LIFE IN GREENLAND ▶

In the AD 980s, Viking leader Eric the Red was exiled from Iceland for murder. He settled on the southwest coast of Greenland where he found green pastures. To encourage other settlers, Eric named the area "Greenland". With good land in Iceland fast running out, boatloads of colonists followed his lead. The Greenlanders traded walrus tusks and polar bear skins for timber, iron, and grain from Norway. The climate was milder then, so the Greenlanders survived easily, but later, the climate changed and the colonies died out.

WALRUS TUSKS

POLAR BEAR

▼ AMERICAN ADVENTURE

The Vikings reached North America centuries before other Europeans arrived. In about AD 986, Bjarni Herjolfsson spotted the coast of America, having been blown off course on a voyage to Greenland. The first actual landing was made by Eric the Red's son, Leif, who arrived in Newfoundland in about AD 1000. The locals resented Eric and the new colonists, so attempts at establishing a permanent settlement were abandoned.

REMAINS OF A VIKING SETTLEMENT AT L'ANSE AUX MEADOWS, NEWFOUNDLAND

DID YOU KNOW?

The Byzantine emperors were so impressed by the Vikings' bravery, that they employed them as their bodyguards. However, when the emperors died, the Viking bodyguards looted their palaces.

Far Horizons

IN THE MIDDLE AGES, the most highly prized luxuries in Europe were spices and silk, which came from the Far East. These goods arrived in the West by a variety of trade routes. These routes were long and tortuous because the most direct routes across Central Asia were blocked by the Muslims. All this changed in the 13th century when the Mongols conquered the region. Trade routes were reopened and merchants were allowed to move freely once more. Meanwhile, the search for quicker, alternative routes to the East encouraged European sailors to undertake dangerous and difficult journeys by sea in their quest for trade and treasure, and to find out more about the world around them.

26–27 SEARCHING FOR ALLIES

In the mid-13th century, the Mongols conquered Central Asia, bringing peace and stability to the region. Merchants from Europe were once more able to travel along the trade routes, which had previously been blocked by the Muslims. European envoys were also sent to the Mongol court in the hope of winning allies against the Muslims.

The founder of the Mongol Empire, Genghis Khan, united the various Mongol groups.

28–29 MARCO POLO

One of the greatest explorers of medieval times, Marco Polo set off from Italy with his father and uncle, travelling along the Silk Road to China. He spent 17 years in the service of the Mongol leader, Kublai Khan, finally returning to Italy in 1295.

Marco Polo saw many new things in China, including metal coins and printed money.

30–31 IBN BATTUTA

In his lifetime, Ibn Battuta covered an astonishing 120,000 km (75,000 miles), visiting places right across the Muslim world and beyond. His account of his travels became one of the greatest geography books of the time.

The dhow was the traditional ship of Arab traders and would have been used by Ibn Battuta on his travels.

32–33 ZHENG HE

The early 15th century saw a new age of Chinese exploration. Admiral Zheng He was appointed by the emperor to lead a series of voyages. With his extraordinary fleet of treasure ships, Zheng He explored large areas of the Pacific and Indian Oceans, greatly increasing Chinese knowledge of the world.

This statue of Zheng He stands in the city of Nanjing, China.

34–35 PORTUGUESE PIONEERS

The great age of European exploration began in the late 15th century with the pioneering voyages of the Portuguese. In their search for a route to the spice markets of Asia, the Portuguese became the first Europeans to reach India by sea.

Some of the spices that lured the Portuguese on their epic journeys.

36–37 HEADING WEST

In his quest for a new sea route to the fabled Spice Islands (the Moluccas), Christopher Columbus sailed west across the Atlantic Ocean. He finally made landfall in the Bahamas, off the coast of North America, but was convinced that he had reached Asia.

The *Santa Maria, Nina,* and *Pinta* – Columbus's three ships from his first voyage.

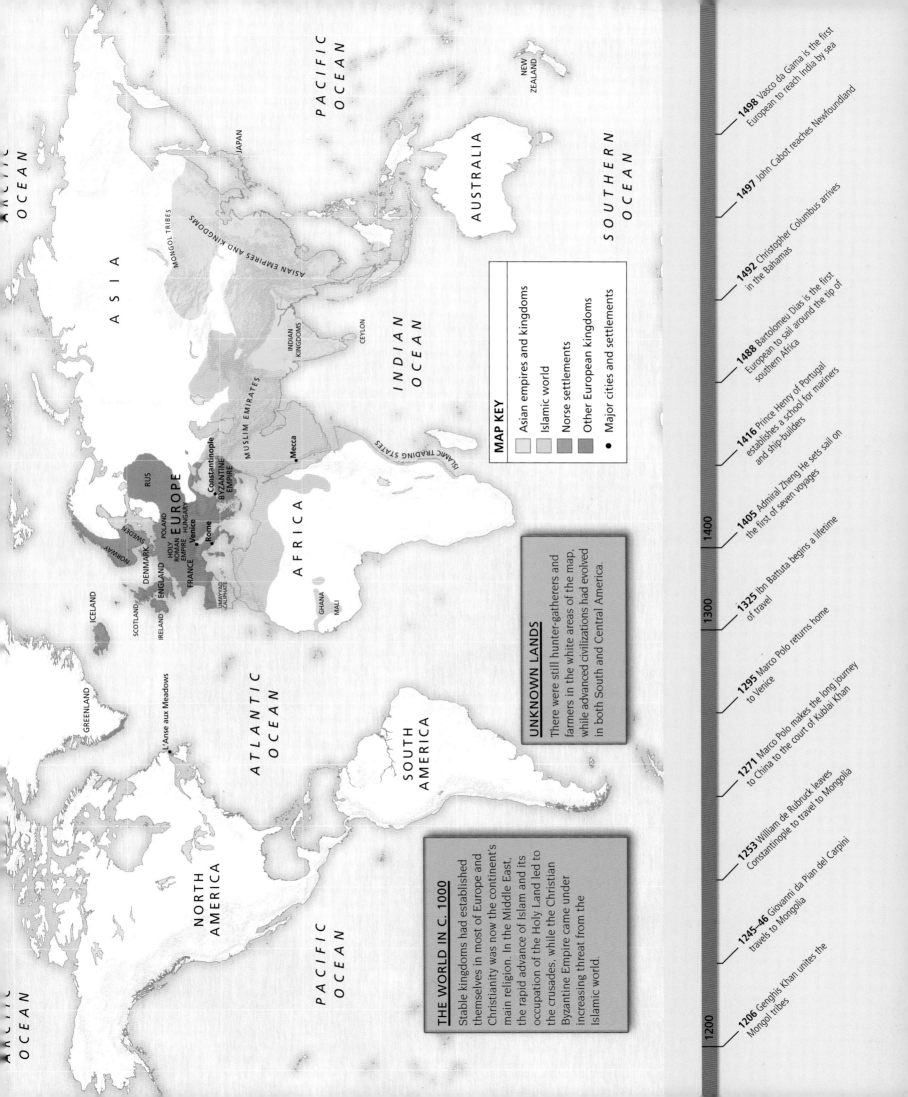

THE WORLD IN C. 1000

Stable kingdoms had established themselves in most of Europe and Christianity was now the continent's main religion. In the Middle East, the rapid advance of Islam and its occupation of the Holy Land led to the crusades, while the Christian Byzantine Empire came under increasing threat from the Islamic world.

UNKNOWN LANDS

There were still hunter-gatherers and farmers in the white areas of the map, while advanced civilizations had evolved in both South and Central America.

MAP KEY

- Asian empires and kingdoms
- Islamic world
- Norse settlements
- Other European kingdoms
- • Major cities and settlements

1498 Vasco da Gama is the first European to reach India by sea

1497 John Cabot reaches Newfoundland

1492 Christopher Columbus arrives in the Bahamas

1488 Bartolomeu Dias is the first European to sail around the tip of southern Africa

1416 Prince Henry of Portugal establishes a school for mariners and ship-builders

1405 Admiral Zheng He sets sail on the first of seven voyages

1325 Ibn Battuta begins a lifetime of travel

1295 Marco Polo returns home to Venice

1271 Marco Polo makes the long journey to China to the court of Kublai Khan

1253 William de Rubruck leaves Constantinople to travel to Mongolia

1245–46 Giovanni da Pian del Carpini travels to Mongolia

1206 Genghis Khan unites the Mongol tribes

1200 1300 1400

Searching for Allies

IN THE MIDDLE AGES, many trade routes across Central Asia were blocked by the Muslims, who had been fighting European Christians in the Middle East. Meanwhile, Mongol hordes had burst upon the scene. At its height, the Mongol empire stretched from modern-day China west into Persia, Russia, Hungary, and Poland. Having made their conquests, the Mongols established law and order, and travel east was again possible. As the Mongols were not hostile to Christians, European kings hoped they might become allies against the Muslims, and sent envoys to court the Khans – and also to find the Christian kingdom of Prester John.

◄ ACROSS ASIA

Mongols (also known as Tartars) were nomadic horsemen from Mongolia. United by Genghis Khan, the Mongols rampaged through Asia, killing and destroying as they went. They were utterly merciless to those who refused to submit to their demands, and are believed to have massacred millions. Their plans to conquer Europe were only abandoned when the second Great Khan Ogedei (Genghis Khan's son) died in 1241.

MAP KEY

← Route of Giovanni da Pian del Carpini (1245–46)
Route of William de Rubruck (1253–55)
← Start to finish route of Pedro de Covilhão (1487–93)

TRAVELS OF A FRIAR ▶

One of the first great Italian travellers was friar Giovanni da Pian del Carpini. In 1245, he was sent as the Pope's personal envoy to the Mongol capital, Karakoram. Carpini travelled mostly on horseback across Europe and into Asia. It took 15 months to reach the Great Khan's court, where he was granted two interviews with Great Khan Guyuk. However, Guyuk's response to the Pope was simply to order his immediate submission.

MONASTERY WALLS in Karakoram, Mongolia, built on the site of the old Mongol capital

SCENE FROM A MAP OF THE WORLD (1375) SHOWS EUROPEAN MERCHANTS JOURNEYING THROUGH ASIA

▲ VISIT TO THE COURT OF KHAN

In 1253, King Louis IX of France sent friar William de Rubruck as a missionary to the Great Khan. The king had heard rumours that the Great Khan had converted to Christianity. After a long and tough journey, travelling by ox cart, de Rubruck reached the court of new Great Khan Mangu. Despite his best efforts, Mangu's only message for the French king was – submit, accept the Khan as overlord, or face war.

CHURCH in Ethiopia was carved from solid rock on the orders of the 13th-century King Lalibela

GENGHIS KHAN

In 1206, a war lord named Temuchin (1155–1227) united the Mongol tribes, taking the name and title Genghis Khan. He led his army to conquer lands that no Mongol had ever seen before.

PRESTER JOHN ▶

In 1167, a letter reached the Pope, supposedly written by Prester ("Priest") John, alleged ruler of a fabulously rich Christian kingdom in the East. The letter was a fake, but people were still searching for the kingdom some 300 years later, hoping its subjects would help their crusade against the Muslims.

▲ ARRIVAL IN ETHIOPIA

The search for Prester John – or his successors – took explorers far afield. At one point, word reached Portugal of a Christian king in Africa and, in 1487, Pedro de Covilhão went to see if it was true. After many hair-raising adventures, he reached Ethiopia. Its king was indeed a Christian, but looked nothing like the Europeans' picture of Prester John. Covilhão remained in Ethiopia as adviser to the king.

Marco Polo

IN 1271, AN EXCITED 16-YEAR-OLD BOY named Marco Polo set off from Venice for China on a journey that would make him one of history's most famous explorers. He travelled with his father and uncle, who were jewel merchants and, thanks to the open policies of the Mongol Khans, had made the journey before. Marco was to spend many years in the service of Great Khan Kublai, ruler of China, whom he came to admire. Kublai Khan was apparently impressed by Marco, too, as he sent him on missions through China and beyond. This gave the young man an unequalled opportunity to explore places such as Sumatra and Java, which were unknown to Europe at that time.

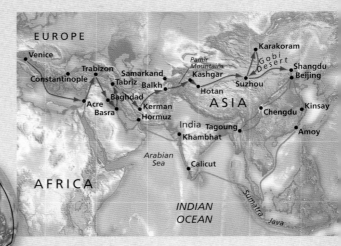

MAP KEY
← Marco Polo's outward journey (1271–75)
← Marco Polo's return journey (1292–95)

CURVED ROOF TOPS were typical of Chinese building styles

▲TRAVELLING EAST
It took the Polos more than three years to reach China. They travelled overland along the old Silk Road – a very dangerous journey. After crossing the treacherous Pamir Mountains, they had to cross the Gobi Desert, which was said to be haunted. They finally reached the Khan's impressive summer palace at Shangdu in 1275.

▲ TRAVELLING SOUTH
During the 17 years that Marco spent in China, he visited various parts of the empire, including the beautiful city of Kinsay. While heading south, he also saw bamboo and ginger plants, and dangerous animals, such as lions, tigers, and bears.

DID YOU KNOW?
The Polo family were able to travel freely on their journeys because they carried "passports" given to them by Kublai Khan. These passports were gold tablets, engraved with words exalting the name of the Khan.

CHINESE PRINTED MONEY) ▶

On his travels across China, Marco saw many extraordinary inventions, such as kites, fireworks, and even paper money, which was unknown in Europe at that time. Paper was first made in China in about AD 105. This led to the invention of paper money and, by the11th century, printed banknotes like this one were in regular use. Paper money was called "flying money" because it tended to fly away in the wind.

METAL COINS shaped like hoes and other tools were used to pay for real tools

▲ RETURN JOURNEY

When the Polos finally decided to return home, Kublai Khan had one last duty for them. They were to escort a Mongolian princess to Persia for her marriage to a Persian chieftain. They set sail in a fleet of Chinese junks in January 1292. After a dreadful voyage lasting two years, they reached Hormuz. Continuing overland, they left the princess in Persia, then embarked for Constantinople. They reached Venice in 1295.

TRAVELLER'S TALES ▶

Three years after arriving home, Marco was arrested by the Genoese, who were at war with Venice. In prison, he met a writer from Pisa, called Rusticello. Marco told him of his travels, and Rusticello wrote the stories down. The collection was called *The Book of Marvels* and later inspired Christopher Columbus to seek out the Far East. Marco only told half of what he had seen though, as no one would have believed everything. This image shows Marco in India where merchants are selling pearls to a prince.

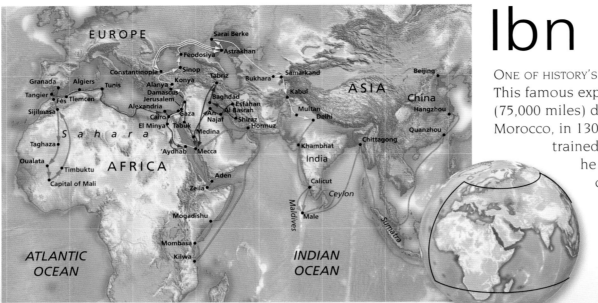

Ibn Battuta

ONE OF HISTORY'S GREAT TRAVELLERS was Ibn Battuta. This famous explorer covered an incredible 120,000 km (75,000 miles) during his lifetime. Born in Tangier, Morocco, in 1304, Battuta was a devout Muslim, who trained in law. After completing his studies, he set off on a pilgrimage to the holy city of Mecca. This trip paved the way for 30 years of travel across the Islamic world. Battuta vowed never to travel the same road twice, but made an exception for his spiritual home of Mecca.

MAP KEY

◄— First stage: Pilgrimage to Mecca 1325–26
◄— Second stage: 1326–27
◄— Third stage: 1327–32
◄— Fourth stage: 1332–34
◄— Fifth stage: 1342–47
◄— Journey through West Africa 1349–54

◄ SACRED PILGRIMAGE

It is the duty of all Muslims to make a pilgrimage to Mecca at least once in their lifetime. In 1325, Battuta travelled along the north African coast, through Egypt and the Middle East, before heading south to Islam's holiest city.

TRIANGULAR SAILS
helped dhows travel close to the wind, enabling them to take more direct routes

SAILING THE SEAS ►

Following his pilgrimage, Battuta travelled to other famous cities, returned to Mecca and studied law for three years. He then embarked on one of the fast Arab dhows and sailed down the east coast of Africa, reaching Mogadishu, Mombasa, and Kilwa.

DID YOU KNOW?

The Sultan of Morocco sent Ibn Battuta a secretary to help him put together an account of his extraordinary travels. This book is now considered to be one of the best sources of knowledge of the world in the 14th century.

▼ IN INDIA

On hearing that the Sultan of Delhi welcomed Muslim scholars to his court, Battuta travelled to India in 1332. Battuta was appointed a grand judge and stayed in India for a few years, before travelling to China to take a position as an ambassador.

QUTUB MINAR, THE SULTAN'S MOSQUE

A FINAL JOURNEY ▶

Almost 25 years after leaving home, Battuta went back to Tangier. His return was brief, because he decided to join a trading caravan and embark on one last journey. Travelling through the Atlas Mountains and the Sahara Desert, he visited the famous city of Timbuktu, with its newly built great mosque, Djingareyber. He stayed for six months before returning north across the Sahara. He arrived home in 1354, his extraordinary travels finally coming to an end.

MUD-WALLED MOSQUE OF DJINGAREYBER, BUILT IN 1327

Zheng He

A NEW AGE OF CHINESE MARITIME VENTURES dawned in the 15th century. Under Emperor Yong Le, the Ming Dynasty (1368–1644) actively encouraged expeditions overseas. Chinese explorers set off in search of new lands where they could assert the country's influence, build relations, and trade. Charismatic sailor and diplomat Admiral Zheng He found favour with the emperor, who sent him on the first of seven incredible voyages in 1405. He commanded an impressive fleet. Huge treasure ships carrying thousands of men and laden with precious goods sailed the seas for years at a time. Many books have been written about these voyages, while towns and temples still bear the name of China's greatest explorer.

PEPPERCORNS AND GINGER from India were valued as much by the Chinese as by Europeans

MAP KEY

⬅ Main routes of Zheng He (1405–33)
⬅ Other places visited by Zheng He
① Destination of Zheng He's seven journeys

◄ CHINESE TRADE

Well before the Ming Dynasty, China had supported and promoted trade. Fruits, spices, gold, ivory, coral, pearls, and rhinoceros horns were the main items sought by the Chinese. Silks and porcelain from China travelled west, either along the Silk Road or in ships to Arabia, and then on to Europe.

◄ EMPEROR'S ORDERS

The Ming Emperor Yong Le, himself a successful conqueror, arranged Zheng He's first journey in 1405. This was a political mission to search for a former emperor, thought to be hiding overseas. He was also told to visit China's neighbouring lands, establish a Chinese presence, and take advantage of trading opportunities. Six similar expeditions followed, all backed by the emperor.

▼ FANTASTIC FLEET

On his first voyage, Zheng He had a fleet of at least 60 wooden ships and many more smaller vessels. Up to 120 m (400 ft) in length, junks were the world's largest ships with nine masts and four decks. They were stronger and better built than their European counterparts, as the Italian explorer Marco Polo noted.

SAILS were staggered so that one sail did not take the wind out of another

DID YOU KNOW?

Altogether, the ships used by Zheng He carried as many as 30,000 men. On board, there were sailors, doctors, scribes, cooks, and horses. Tubs of earth were taken, too, and kept on deck for growing vegetables and fruits.

FAR AND WIDE ▶

During his first three voyages, Zheng He reached southeast Asia, India, and Ceylon (modern Sri Lanka). His fourth expedition sailed as far as Arabia and the Persian Gulf, while later voyages ventured down the east African coast to Malindi (in modern Kenya). By the time the last fleet returned home in 1433, Zheng He's expeditions had greatly increased Chinese knowledge of the world beyond its shores. Besides his many diplomatic successes, Zheng He brought home treasures, animals, and plants never before seen in China. One African ruler sent the Chinese emperor a giraffe as a gift.

STATUE OF ZHENG HE IN NANJING

◀ CLOSED COUNTRY

After Emperor Yong Le died in 1424, his successors were suspicious about overseas trade. They believed that China produced everything it required, so there was no need to buy from abroad. Orders were issued banning foreign trade and travel. Any Chinese merchant caught trading overseas was declared a pirate and executed. Zheng He fell from favour and probably died on his last voyage in 1433. The treasure ships were abandoned in harbours, where they rotted away.

Portuguese Pioneers

By the 15th century, European merchants were searching for new sea routes that would lead them to the valuable markets of the East. Enter Prince Henry of Portugal, a man with a mission. His long-term plan was to train a whole generation of expert sailors and navigators, capable of sailing around Africa to India and beyond. Potential profits for those who controlled the sea routes were so huge that each new discovery and map were kept top secret. As Henry's sailors set off on a series of daring voyages south into unknown seas, the great age of European exploration was underway.

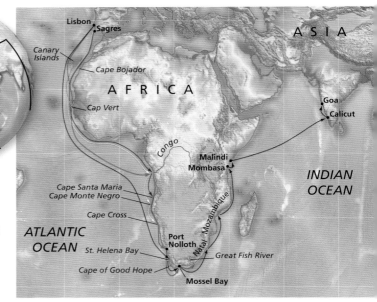

MAP KEY

← Voyage of Gil Eannes (1433)
← First voyage of Diogo Cão (1482–84)
← Second voyage of Diogo Cão (1485–86)
← Voyage of Bartolomeu Dias (1487–88)
← First voyage of Vasco da Gama (1497–98)

◀ PRINCE HENRY

As a young man, Henry had been part of an expedition to stamp out pirates, but in 1416 he established a school for navigators, map makers, and ship-builders at Sagres, on the southwest coast of Portugal. Although Henry never sailed on these expeditions himself, he was known as "The Navigator" because he inspired others to explore and sponsored many expeditions that travelled further and further south.

AROUND AFRICA ▶

Sailing south took courage as most people believed there was dense fog, boiling sea, and burning land towards the equator. The breakthrough came in 1433 when Gil Eannes rounded Cape Bojador without encountering such hazards. On his two expeditions, Diogo Cão pressed further south then any previous European, exploring the River Congo and Cape Cross.

▲ CAPE OF GOOD HOPE

Three years after Cão's voyage, Portuguese navigator Bartolomeu Dias became the first European explorer to sail around the Cape of Good Hope at the southern tip of Africa, and into the Indian Ocean. Dias wanted to continue his journey to India, but his exhausted crew had other ideas. With supplies running short, they signed a petition, forcing Dias to head home.

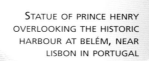

STATUE OF PRINCE HENRY OVERLOOKING THE HISTORIC HARBOUR AT BELÉM, NEAR LISBON IN PORTUGAL

NUTMEG

CLOVES

CINNAMON

PEPPERCORNS

◀ CARAVELS

The exciting voyages of the
Portuguese were made possible
by the development of a new
type of sailing ship, called
a caravel. These vessels
were only about 20 m
(66 ft) in length, making
them highly manoeuvrable.
Early caravels, like this
one, had triangular sails for
sailing close to the coast. Later
types had square sails, which made them
faster on the open ocean.

REACHING INDIA ▶

Following the success of Dias,
the Portuguese sent a trading
expedition to India. It was led by
Vasco da Gama, who set sail from
Lisbon in 1497 with four ships and
150 men. A year later, da Gama
reached Calicut on the west coast
of India, becoming the first
European to reach India by sea.
However, he failed to establish
satisfactory trading links with
India as Arab merchants were
already in control of the trade.

THE SPICE TRADE ▶

In Europe, spices, such as
nutmeg, cloves, cinnamon,
and peppercorns, were used
to add flavour to food. These
precious spices only grew far away in
the East, in India, Ceylon (Sri Lanka),
and the fabled Spice Islands (the Moluccas).
To reach Europe, they had to be transported
thousands of kilometres, but the potential
rewards were substantial. Once the route
was opened, Spanish, English, and
Dutch merchants challenged
Portugal's trading empire.

DUG-OUT CANOES
ON THE RIVER CONGO

DID YOU KNOW?

To mark their progress along the coast
and establish their claim to land, the
Portuguese set up stone pillars, called
padrãos. Each pillar was inscribed
with a cross and the Portuguese
coat of arms.

Heading West

WHILE THE PORTUGUESE PIONEERS searched for an eastern sea route to the Indies, two Italian explorers headed in the opposite direction. The famous navigator Christopher Columbus hatched a plan to find eastern lands by travelling west. In 1492, he set sail from Spain on the first of four voyages across the Atlantic. Five years later, the mariner John Cabot also tried to find Asia by sailing west from England. Although neither of them reached Asia, both discovered new lands, with Columbus finding the Americas and Cabot reaching Newfoundland.

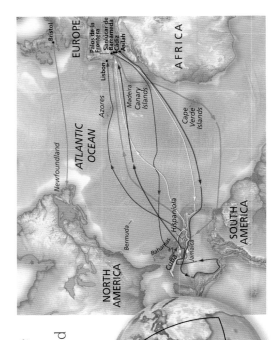

MAP KEY

↓	First voyage of Columbus (1492–93)
↯	Second voyage of Columbus (1493–96)
↓	Third voyage of Columbus (1498–1500)
↓	Fourth voyage of Columbus (1502–04)
↓	First voyage of John Cabot (1497)

▼ SMALL SHIPS

On his first voyage, Columbus took three ships – *Nina*, *Pinta*, and his flagship *Santa Maria*. With three masts and square sails, *Santa Maria* was designed to move quickly in the strong Atlantic winds. Despite being the largest of the three, the ship was only 30 m (100 ft) in length. Space was limited, so the crew of 40 slept and cooked on deck, while Columbus had the luxury of a small cabin with a bunk bed.

DID YOU KNOW?

Most historians believe that the Americas were named after Amerigo Vespucci. Others, however, claim that it was named after Richard Amerike, an English customs officer who helped finance John Cabot.

JOHN CABOT preparing to board his ship *Matthew* and embark on his first voyage

▲ CABOT'S LAND

Like Columbus, the Italian John Cabot believed it was possible to reach Asia by travelling west. He left England in 1497 and reached Newfoundland, but convinced himself it was China. Many European fishermen followed Cabot's route, attracted by his accounts of plentiful fish stocks.

▼ NEW DISCOVERIES

During his second voyage, Columbus arrived in Cuba, despite firmly believing that the island was part of mainland Asia. It was here that Columbus first tasted pineapples. Columbus and his crew discovered many new kinds of food on their travels, including sweet potatoes and sweetcorn. The sailors also came across hammocks, which were subsequently widely used on board the ships.

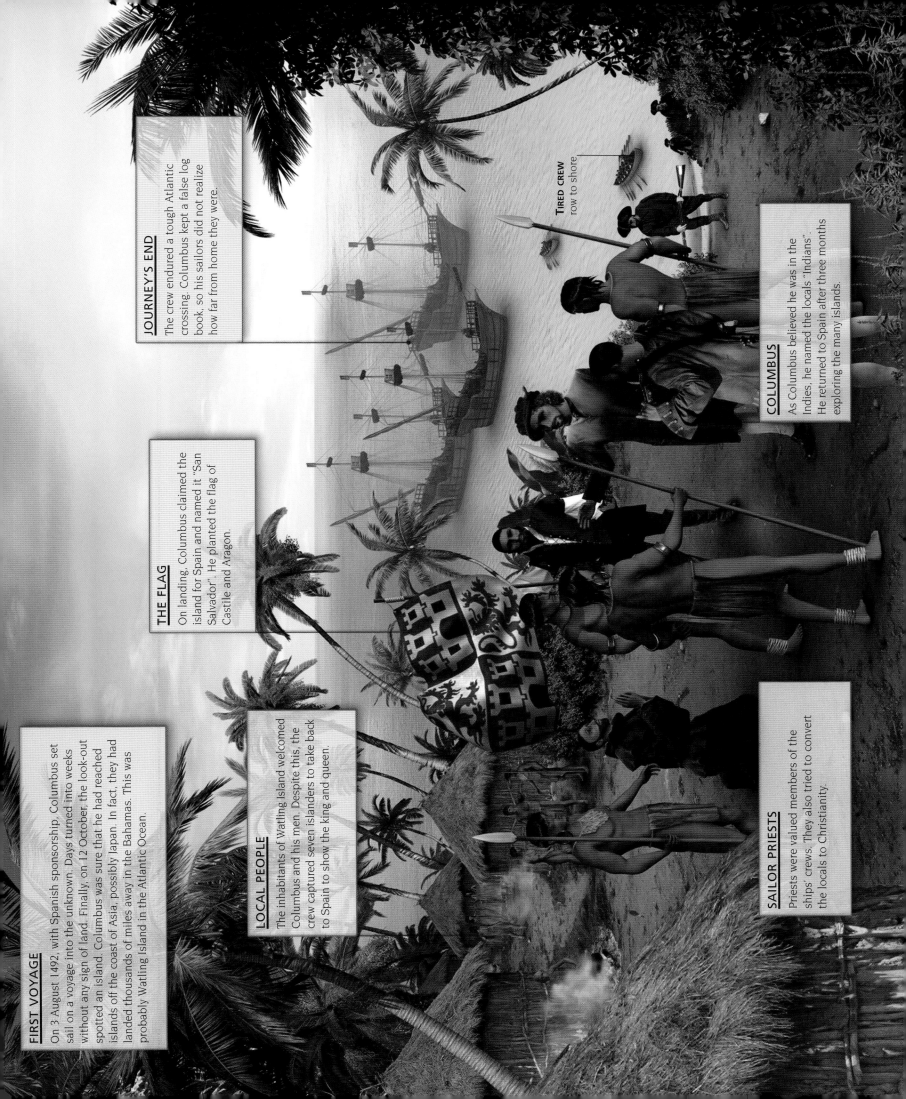

FIRST VOYAGE

On 3 August 1492, with Spanish sponsorship, Columbus set sail on a voyage into the unknown. Days turned into weeks without any sign of land. Finally, on 12 October, the look-out spotted an island. Columbus was sure that he had reached islands off the coast of Asia, possibly Japan. In fact, they had landed thousands of miles away in the Bahamas. This was probably Watling Island in the Atlantic Ocean.

LOCAL PEOPLE

The inhabitants of Watling Island welcomed Columbus and his men. Despite this, the crew captured seven islanders to take back to Spain to show the king and queen.

SAILOR PRIESTS

Priests were valued members of the ships' crews. They also tried to convert the locals to Christianity.

THE FLAG

On landing, Columbus claimed the island for Spain and named it "San Salvador". He planted the flag of Castile and Aragon.

JOURNEY'S END

The crew endured a tough Atlantic crossing. Columbus kept a false log book, so his sailors did not realize how far from home they were.

TIRED CREW
row to shore

COLUMBUS

As Columbus believed he was in the Indies, he named the locals "Indians". He returned to Spain after three months exploring the many islands.

Exploration and Conquest

IN THE 16TH AND 17TH CENTURIES, trade remained the motive behind some of the most intrepid voyages of the time. The search for the Northeast and Northwest Passages – alternative and quicker routes to the riches of Asia – led explorers through some of the most treacherous seas on the planet. Such exploration was also aided by advances in ship building and navigational tools. Exploration for trade, however, was now closely followed by conquest. In the New World, French explorers opened up North America for trade and settlement, while in South America, Spanish conquistadors, driven by their desire for gold, defeated the Aztec and Inca Empires.

40–41 AROUND THE WORLD

The first two expeditions to sail around the world were led by Ferdinand Magellan in 1519 and Francis Drake in 1577. These expeditions provided valuable information about the size of the world and the position of the continents.

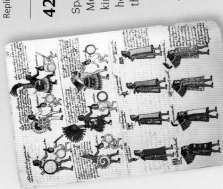

Replica of Drake's flagship, the *Golden Hind*.

42–43 CORTÉS IN MEXICO

Spanish conquistador Hernán Cortés reached Mexico in 1519, spurred on by rumours of kingdoms rich in gold. Within a few years, he and his men had destroyed the Aztec Empire, then at the height of its power and wealth.

A page from an Aztec book called a codex, which recorded the life of the Aztecs.

44–45 PIZARRO IN PERU

More tales of gold prompted the invasion of the Inca Empire by Francisco Pizarro in 1531. Despite their bravery and their mountain hideouts, the Incas were conquered.

One of the few surviving Inca items of gold.

46–47 SOUTH AMERICA

Driven by their greed for gold, the Spaniards and Portuguese sent further expeditions to explore South America.

Mountains, deserts, and rainforests in South America were formidable barriers to exploration.

48–49 NORTH AMERICA

In the 16th century, French and Spanish explorers began to open up North America for trade and settlement. In the north, the French searched for a waterway to the Pacific Ocean, while the Spaniards explored further south.

The Grand Canyon in the USA was first seen by Europeans in the 1540s.

50–51 NORTHEAST PASSAGE

Many explorers set out to find a quicker route to China along Russia's ice-bound north coast. It was not until the late 19th century, however, that a passage was finally found.

Today, icebreakers keep the Northeast Passage clear.

52–53 NORTHWEST PASSAGE

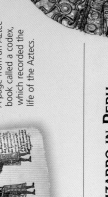

In the late 16th century, the English took the lead in searching for the passage that links the Atlantic and Pacific Oceans across the top of North America.

A backstaff was used to calculate latitude.

54–55 PACIFIC PIONEERS

The exploration of the Pacific Ocean was driven by trade and also curiosity – explorers were eager to find out if a southern continent existed.

Spices grew only in the Far East and so were very expensive.

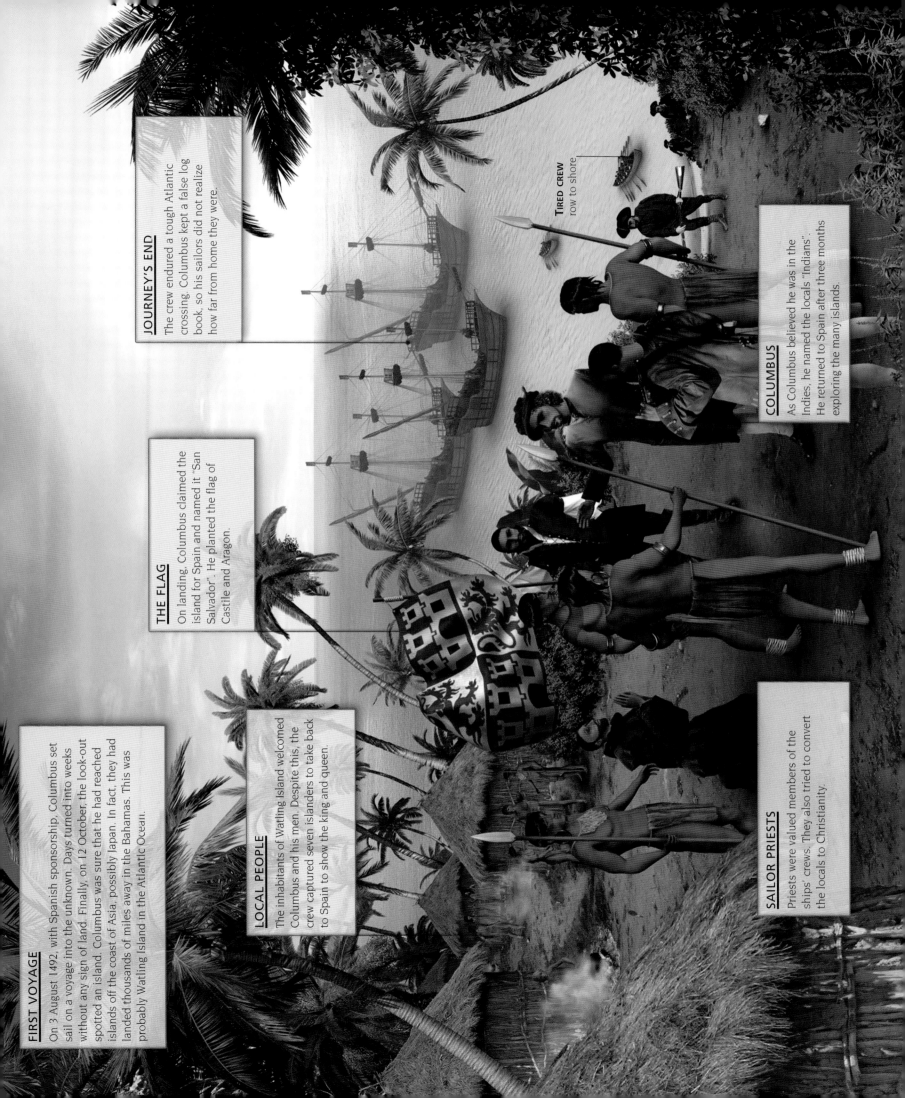

FIRST VOYAGE

On 3 August 1492, with Spanish sponsorship, Columbus set sail on a voyage into the unknown. Days turned into weeks without any sign of land. Finally, on 12 October, the look-out spotted an island. Columbus was sure that he had reached islands off the coast of Asia, possibly Japan. In fact, they had landed thousands of miles away in the Bahamas. This was probably Watling Island in the Atlantic Ocean.

LOCAL PEOPLE

The inhabitants of Watling Island welcomed Columbus and his men. Despite this, the crew captured seven islanders to take back to Spain to show the king and queen.

SAILOR PRIESTS

Priests were valued members of the ships' crews. They also tried to convert the locals to Christianity.

JOURNEY'S END

The crew endured a tough Atlantic crossing. Columbus kept a false log book, so his sailors did not realize how far from home they were.

THE FLAG

On landing, Columbus claimed the island for Spain and named it "San Salvador". He planted the flag of Castile and Aragon.

TIRED CREW
row to shore

COLUMBUS

As Columbus believed he was in the Indies, he named the locals "Indians". He returned to Spain after three months exploring the many islands.

Exploration and Conquest

In the 16th and 17th centuries, trade remained the motive behind some of the most intrepid voyages of the time. The search for the Northeast and Northwest Passages – alternative and quicker routes to the riches of Asia – led explorers through some of the most treacherous seas on the planet. Such exploration was also aided by advances in ship building and navigational tools. Exploration for trade, however, was now closely followed by conquest. In the New World, French explorers opened up North America for trade and settlement, while in South America, Spanish conquistadors, driven by their desire for gold, defeated the Aztec and Inca Empires.

40–41 Around the World

The first two expeditions to sail around the world were led by Ferdinand Magellan in 1519 and Francis Drake in 1577. These expeditions provided valuable information about the size of the world and the position of the continents.

Replica of Drake's flagship, the *Golden Hind*.

42–43 Cortés in Mexico

Spanish conquistador Hernán Cortés reached Mexico in 1519, spurred on by rumours of kingdoms rich in gold. Within a few years, he and his men had destroyed the Aztec Empire, then at the height of its power and wealth.

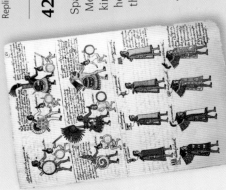

A page from an Aztec book called a codex, which recorded the life of the Aztecs.

44–45 Pizarro in Peru

More tales of gold prompted the invasion of the Inca Empire by Francisco Pizarro in 1531. Despite their bravery and their mountain hideouts, the Incas were conquered.

One of the few surviving Inca items of gold.

46–47 South America

Driven by their greed for gold, the Spaniards and Portuguese sent further expeditions to explore South America.

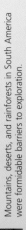

Mountains, deserts, and rainforests in South America were formidable barriers to exploration.

48–49 North America

In the 16th century, French and Spanish explorers began to open up North America for trade and settlement. In the north, the French searched for a waterway to the Pacific Ocean, while the Spaniards explored further south.

The Grand Canyon in the USA was first seen by Europeans in the 1540s.

50–51 Northeast Passage

Many explorers set out to find a quicker route to China along Russia's ice-bound north coast. It was not until the late 19th century, however, that a passage was finally found.

Today, icebreakers keep the Northeast Passage clear.

Spices grew only in the Far East and so were very expensive.

52–53 Northwest Passage

In the late 16th century, the English took the lead in searching for the passage that links the Atlantic and Pacific Oceans across the top of North America.

54–55 Pacific Pioneers

The exploration of the Pacific Ocean was driven by trade and also curiosity – explorers were eager to find out if a southern continent existed.

A backstaff was used to calculate latitude.

MAP KEY

- Asian kingdoms
- China (Ming Empire)
- England and possessions
- Indian kingdoms
- Islamic world and other trading states
- Russia
- Portugal and possessions
- Spain and possessions
- Denmark and possessions
- Other European kingdoms
- Major cities

THE PACIFIC

Although New Zealand, Australia, and the Pacific Islands were inhabited, their existence was not known to Europeans.

THE WORLD IN C. 1500

Through trade and travel, Europe had built up a limited knowledge of Asia and North Africa. The Islamic world stretched across three continents, but little was still known about the white areas of this map – the existence of the Australian continent was completely unknown, and there were still vast areas of Asia, Africa, and North and South America to be explored.

OCEANS AND SEAS

PACIFIC OCEAN
ARCTIC OCEAN
ATLANTIC OCEAN
INDIAN OCEAN
SOUTHERN OCEAN

CONTINENTS AND REGIONS

NORTH AMERICA
SOUTH AMERICA
AFRICA
EUROPE
ASIA
AUSTRALIA
ASIAN KINGDOMS
CHINA (MING EMPIRE)
INDIAN KINGDOMS
ISLAMIC WORLD
ISLAMIC AND OTHER TRADING STATES
OTTOMAN EMPIRE
HOLY ROMAN EMPIRE
RUSSIA
NORWAY
SWEDEN
DENMARK
ENGLAND
FRANCE
PORTUGAL
SPAIN

PLACES

GREENLAND
ICELAND
Newfoundland
West Indies
Azores
Canary Islands
Madeira
Cape Verde
São Tomé and Príncipe
Moscow
Copenhagen
London
Madrid
Lisbon
Venice
Rome
Constantinople
Mecca
Beijing
CEYLON
JAPAN
TASMANIA
NEW ZEALAND

TIMELINE

1500

1513 Vasco Núñez de Balboa becomes the first European to see the Pacific Ocean

1519 Ferdinand Magellan leads the first expedition to sail around the world

1521 Hernán Cortés conquers the Aztecs

1532 Francisco Pizarro conquers the Incas

1534 Jacques Cartier reaches the Gulf of St Lawrence, Canada

1541–42 Francisco de Orellana sails the length of the Amazon River

1540 Coronado and Cárdenas start to explore southwest of North America

1576 Martin Frobisher seeks the Northwest Passage

1580 Francis Drake completes the second circumnavigation of the world

1600

1596 Willem Barents sets off to find the Northeast Passage

1610 Henry Hudson discovers Hudson Bay

1642 Abel Tasman sails past Tasmania and discovers New Zealand

Around the World

SPAIN AND PORTUGAL WERE NOW bitter rivals in the race to explore, to found colonies abroad, and to claim authority over the Spice Islands (the Moluccas). To settle this rivalry, the Pope negoiated the Treaty of Tordesillas in 1494. To the west of an imaginary line through the Atlantic was to be Spain's sphere of influence, and to the east was Portugal's. However, many people were not happy with the arrangement. Ferdinand Magellan, a Portuguese gentleman in the service of Spain, proposed a plan. He would sail around South America and west across the Pacific Ocean to the Spice Islands and thus claim them for Spain. However, storms, mutiny, and disease inflicted terrible losses, and Magellan himself was killed. It was some 50 years before another daring seaman, Francis Drake, achieved the second circumnavigation of the world.

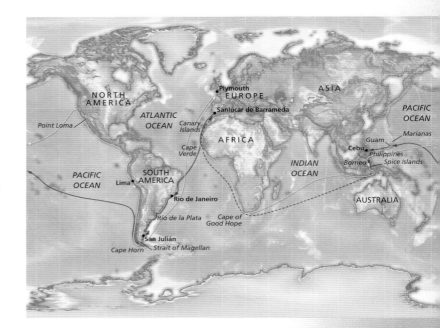

MAP KEY

→ Voyage of Ferdinand Magellan (1519–21)
◄- - Return of Magellan's crew after his death (1521–22)
⇦ Voyage of Francis Drake (1577–80)

◄ **EXOTIC GOODS**

Magellan set sail from Spain in September 1519, with a fleet of five ships and some 260 men, to search for the Spice Islands. He first sailed south to the Canary Islands, where the ships took on fresh supplies of water and food, then along the coast of West Africa, taking care to avoid any Portuguese patrols. Magellan next turned westward and crossed the Atlantic Ocean, continuing along the South American coast. By March 1520, the fleet had reached the bay of San Julián (in modern Argentina), where they spent the southern winter.

TALKING PARROTS, along with spices, gems, and silks, could be bought in the Spice Islands

Ferdinand Magellan

As a young adventurer, Ferdinand Magellan (1480–1521) served the Portuguese royal family, and went on several expeditions. However, feeling his efforts were not fully appreciated, Magellan entered the service of the King of Spain in 1514.

◄ **STRAIT OF MAGELLAN**

In September 1520, at the start of spring in the southern hemisphere, the fleet continued south. During stormy weather, two of Magellan's ships were blown into a deep-water channel, but returned with exciting news. They had found the fabled passage, now known as the Strait of Magellan, which linked the Atlantic and Pacific Oceans. A month later, Magellan sailed out into the world's largest ocean.

MAST – galleons were sailing ships with three (or four) masts

CROW'S NEST is where a sailor worked the sails – high rails were to keep him safe

DEATH OF MAGELLAN ▲

Magellan had underestimated the distance to the Spice Islands, and without fresh food and water, many men died of starvation and disease. In March 1521, the remaining crew reached Guam, then sailed on to the Philippines, where Magellan was killed in a battle between two of the islands. Under the command of Juan Sebastián de Elcano, the two remaining ships – the *Trinidad* and the *Vittoria* – reached the Spice Islands and loaded up with spices and other luxuries. In September 1522, the *Vittoria* limped back to Spain alone. Of the original company, only 18 men survived.

MODERN REPLICA OF DRAKE'S SHIP, THE *GOLDEN HIND*

◄ DRAKE'S JOURNEY

English sea captain Francis Drake led the second circumnavigation of the globe. Backed by Queen Elizabeth I, Drake set sail in 1577. The main reason for Drake's voyage was not exploration but to claim new territories for the crown and to plunder Spanish treasure ships. Even so, Drake made several important discoveries. He found that open ocean lay to the south of Cape Horn, proving that South America was not linked to another continent to the south. He also sailed further north up the western coast of America than any previous explorer.

Cortés in Mexico

THE MIGHTY AZTEC EMPIRE flourished during the 1400s. It covered roughly the area that is now Mexico, and was one of the most developed civilizations on this continent. The emperor dominated his people, and religion played an important part in everyday life. During the early 1500s, rumours reached the Spanish colonies in the West Indies that told of civilizations on the mainland, which were fabulously rich in gold. So in 1519, Diego de Velásquez, governor of Cuba, appointed Hernán Cortés to lead an expedition. Within two years of his arrival, the Aztec Empire had been conquered for Spain.

NORTH AMERICA

Gulf of Mexico

Cabo Rojo
Chichén-Itzá
Cuba
Tenochtitlán Cempoala Campeche
San Juan de Ulúa
Isla Cozumel
Tulúm
Champotón
Cintla
Coatzacoalcos

Caribbean Sea

PACIFIC OCEAN

MAP KEY

← Hernán Cortés's route to Tenochtitlán (1519)

HORSES were shipped from Spain, and were unknown to the Aztecs

CORTÉS
When Cortés arrived on the east coast, he burned his ships so that there could be no turning back for his men. Then he marched towards the Aztec capital of Tenochtitlán.

DOÑA MARINA was an Aztec girl who helped Cortés as a translator and advisor

ARRIVAL IN TENOCHTITLÁN
Tenochtitlán was built on an island in Lake Texcoco. By the time of the Spanish conquest, it was home to some 300,000 people. Cortés led his army into the city, then left to fetch allies. When he returned, he laid siege to the city, cutting off its food and water supplies, and forcing the Aztecs to surrender.

EMPEROR MONTEZUMA
At first, Montezuma welcomed Cortés. But as time passed, the Aztecs realized Cortés's intentions were not peaceful.

AZTEC GOLD ▶
When Cortés arrived in Mexico, the Aztec Empire was at its height. From Tenochtitlán, the Aztec emperor ruled over five million people. Part of the Spaniards' mission was to claim the region for Spain and convert the Aztecs to Christianity. Their main driving force, however, was their greed for Aztec gold. Many exquisite gold objects were melted down and turned into coins, which the Spaniards shipped home.

Hernán Cortés

The son of a Spanish nobleman, Hernán Cortés (1485–1547) studied law at Salamanca University. However, he abandoned his studies to seek his fortune in the New World. In Cuba, he was appointed secretary to the governor, who sent him to Mexico. With a party of only about 600 men, Cortés brought the Aztec civilization to an end.

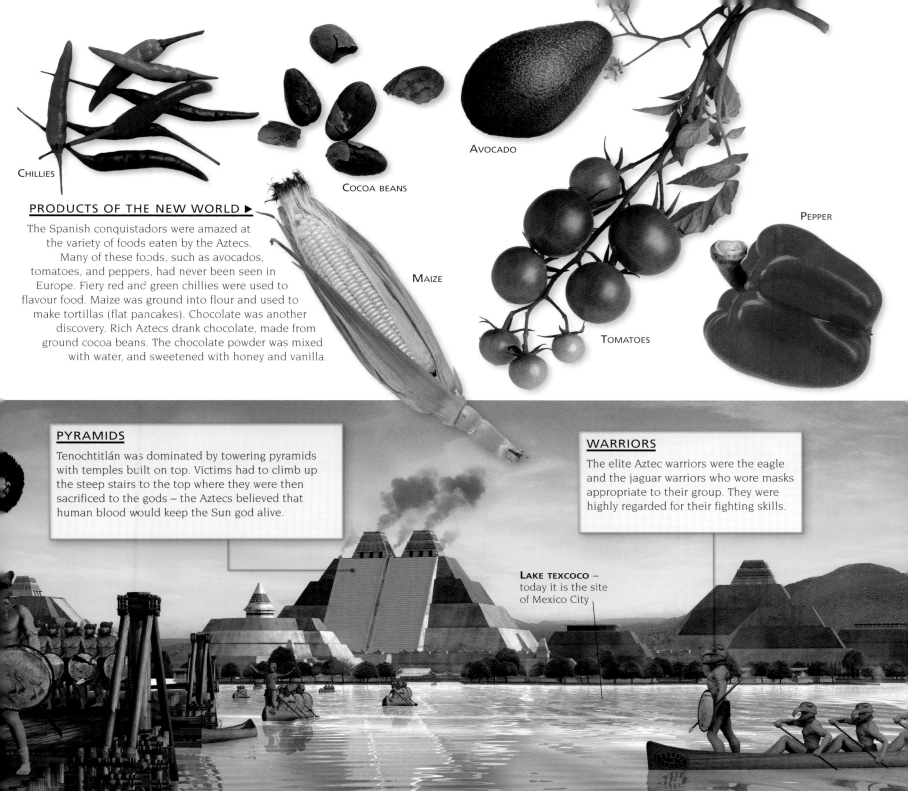

CHILLIES

COCOA BEANS

AVOCADO

MAIZE

PEPPER

TOMATOES

PRODUCTS OF THE NEW WORLD ▶

The Spanish conquistadors were amazed at the variety of foods eaten by the Aztecs. Many of these foods, such as avocados, tomatoes, and peppers, had never been seen in Europe. Fiery red and green chillies were used to flavour food. Maize was ground into flour and used to make tortillas (flat pancakes). Chocolate was another discovery. Rich Aztecs drank chocolate, made from ground cocoa beans. The chocolate powder was mixed with water, and sweetened with honey and vanilla.

PYRAMIDS

Tenochtitlán was dominated by towering pyramids with temples built on top. Victims had to climb up the steep stairs to the top where they were then sacrificed to the gods – the Aztecs believed that human blood would keep the Sun god alive.

WARRIORS

The elite Aztec warriors were the eagle and the jaguar warriors who wore masks appropriate to their group. They were highly regarded for their fighting skills.

LAKE TEXCOCO – today it is the site of Mexico City

AZTEC CODEX ▶

The Aztecs recorded their history, myths, customs, and details of their daily lives in folded books called codices. They were painted on strips of bark, agave (cactus) paper, or deerskin. The page from a codex on the right shows Aztec warriors taking prisoners. The more successful a warrior was, the more elaborate a costume he was entitled to wear. Unfortunately, many of the codices were destroyed by the Spaniards. The few in existence are thought to be copies made after the Spanish conquest.

AZTEC FISHING FROM A BOAT

AZTEC MARRIAGE CEREMONY

Pizarro in Peru

THE AZTECS WERE NOT THE ONLY ancient civilization to feel the full force of the conquistadors. Cortés's expedition to Mexico inspired the conquest of another ancient civilization of the New World. Further south, the immensely wealthy Inca Empire covered a vast territory, stretching for thousands of kilometres down the west coast of South America. The man chosen to search for the Incas was Francisco Pizarro. Like Cortés, he invaded an unknown land with only a handful of men. Within three years of landing in Peru, Pizarro had destroyed the Inca Empire.

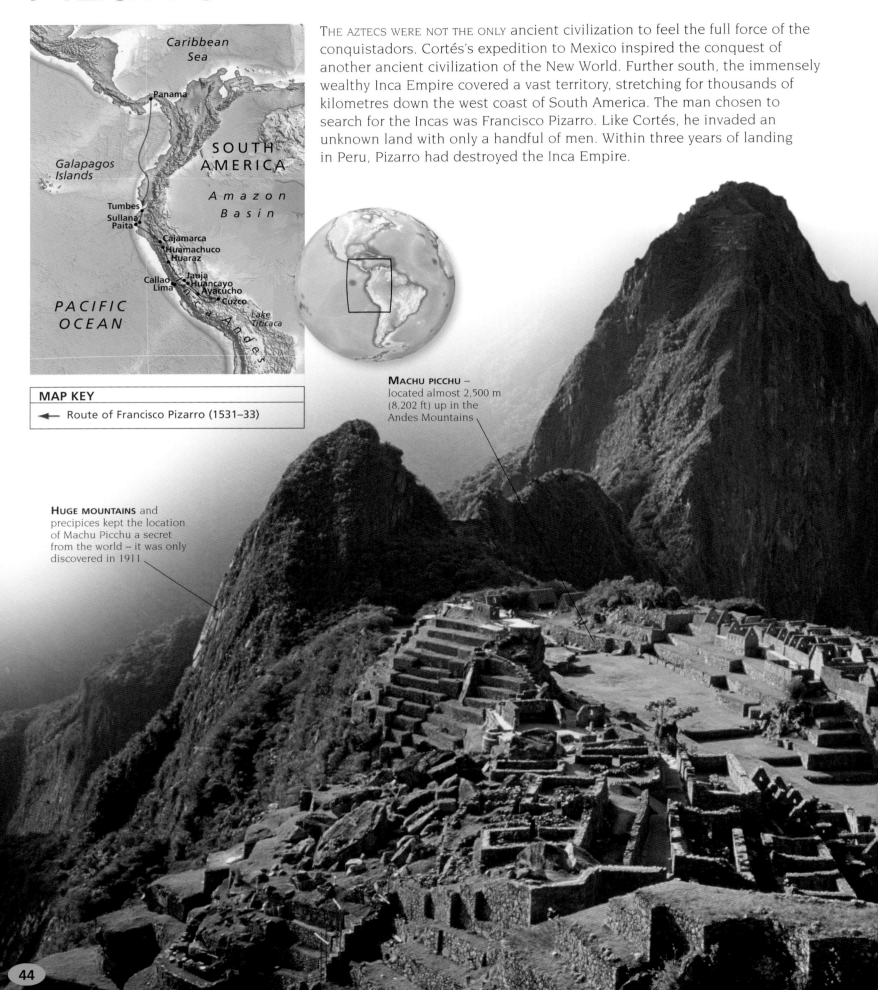

MAP KEY

← Route of Francisco Pizarro (1531–33)

MACHU PICCHU – located almost 2,500 m (8,202 ft) up in the Andes Mountains

HUGE MOUNTAINS and precipices kept the location of Machu Picchu a secret from the world – it was only discovered in 1911

◄ A GOLDEN EMPIRE

Different parts of the vast Inca Empire were linked by an extraordinary network of roads and bridges. The empire was strictly controlled by the Inca emperor, who was believed to have descended from the Sun god. The empire was also fabulously rich in gold – in Cuzco itself, the capital city, the Temple of the Sun was said to be covered in gold and silver.

INCA GOLD OBJECT
SHOWING THE SUN GOD

BATTLE AT CAJAMARCA ▲

In 1532, Pizarro reached northern Peru. With no more than 170 troops and a few horses, he marched inland, and advanced to Cajamarca, where Emperor Atahualpa and his huge army were waiting to meet him. A Spanish priest offered a Bible to the emperor but he refused it. Using this as an excuse, the Spaniards attacked, and took Atahualpa prisoner.

A FORTRESS CITY

With Atahualpa held hostage, Pizarro seized Cajamarca for Spain. To secure his release, Atahualpa offered to fill a room with gold and silver. Pizarro took the treasure, but still had the emperor put to death. The Spaniards then marched on Cuzco, the richest city in the empire. After a bloody battle in which thousands of Incas were killed, the Spaniards forced the survivors to surrender their gold. Some of the Incas managed to escape to the mountain strongholds like Machu Picchu, which the conquistadors never discovered.

Francisco Pizarro

Soldier's son, Francisco Pizarro (c. 1475–1541) served in the Spanish army before sailing to the West Indies in 1502. Over the next 20 years, he took part in several expeditions. When Pizarro defeated the Inca Empire, he fell out with fellow conquistador, Diego de Almagro. He was killed by de Almagro's men.

FATE OF THE INCAS ▲

The Spaniards destroyed the Incas and their culture. Many were killed or died from smallpox and other diseases contracted from the Spaniards. Others were forced to work in the gold and silver mines. Most of the looted golden treasure was melted down by the Spaniards and made into coins. Very little remained of the old Inca Empire. Today, the descendants of the Incas are still proud of their great heritage.

South America

FOLLOWING CHRISTOPHER COLUMBUS'S VOYAGES, other European explorers set sail across the Atlantic Ocean for the New World. Still convinced that they would find a passage to the Indian Ocean and the Spice Islands (the Moluccas), the Spaniards occupied the islands we now call the West Indies. However, Magellan's voyage had shown the vast size of South America, so interest turned to exploring the new continent. Driven by the quest for gold, the Spaniards and Portuguese sent out expeditions to explore the South American mainland. At first, these expeditions kept close to the coast for safety. Some did venture inland, but the difficult terrain meant that much of South America remained a mystery.

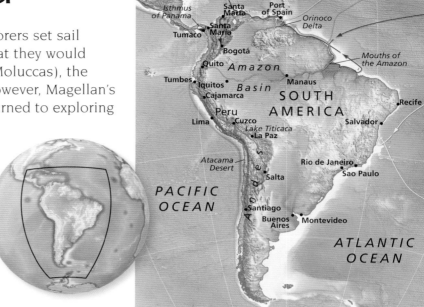

◄ ENTER THE PORTUGUESE

Italian-born navigator Amerigo Vespucci sailed on several Spanish and Portuguese expeditions to South America. In 1499, he reached Venezuela and the mouth of the Orinoco River. A year later, Pedro Alvares Cabral became the first European to reach Brazil, having been blown off course in the Atlantic. He claimed the country for Portugal.

AMERIGO VESPUCCI

MAP KEY

◄— Route of Amerigo Vespucci (1499–1500)
⤙— Route of Pedro Alvarez Cabral (1500)
◄— Route of Vasco Núñez de Balboa (1513)
◄— Route of Diego de Almagro (1535–37)
◄— Route of Francisco de Orellana (1541–42)
◄— Route of Gonzalo Jimenez de Quesada (1536–37)
◄┈┈ First voyage of Sir Walter Raleigh (1595)
◄— Second voyage of Sir Walter Raleigh (1617)

DE ALMAGRO IN CHILE ▼

Diego de Almagro left Cuzco in 1535 after helping Francisco Pizarro defeat the Incas, intending to explore the region further south. After an eight-month march to Argentina, he crossed the Andes into Chile, losing many men on the way. Finding no gold, he decided to return to Peru, first crossing the Atacama Desert, the driest place on Earth.

SNOWCAPPED VOLCANOES tower above the parched desert sand

DID YOU KNOW?

Spain already held large areas of Europe, and its American empire made it the greatest and richest power of the 16th century. It was the Aztec and the Inca gold that paid for Spanish wars in Europe, and turned Spain into a formidable force.

RAINFOREST growing on the banks of the River Amazon

▲ EXPLORING THE AMAZON

In 1541, explorers Gonzalo Pizarro and Francisco de Orellana set out on an expedition from Ecuador. But provisions ran out and the party split into two, with de Orellana forging ahead to find food. He discovered a river, naming it the Amazon after a tribe of legendary women warriors, and sailed more than 4,000 km (2,500 miles) along it before heading back to Spain. Pizarro and his men were forced to retrace their route, living off snakes, insects, and their own leather belts.

◀ ALBOA IN THE PACIFIC ▶

In 1510, Spanish conquistador Vasco Núñez de Balboa settled in Santa María (in modern-day Panama). From there, he set out in search of a great sea, reported to be rich in gold. In 1513, after a difficult journey through thick rainforest, Balboa crossed the Isthmus of Panama and saw the Pacific Ocean for the first time. Balboa was planning an expedition to explore the sea for gold when he was killed.

BALBOA raising his sword to claim the Pacific Ocean and its coasts for Spain

GOLD MODEL OF THE KING OF GUATAVITA ON HIS RAFT

EL DORADO ▶

The search for gold led many explorers to journey through South America. One of these was Gonzalo Jimenez de Quesada, who explored modern-day Colombia. The explorers brought back stories of El Dorado – a king who boarded a raft once a year to throw gold and jewels into Lake Guatavita, near Bogotá. Later, El Dorado was believed to be a golden city, hidden deep in the rainforest. English sailor Sir Walter Raleigh was one of many who tried and failed to find it on his expeditions of 1595 and 1617.

North America

In the 16th century, fleets of European fishing boats sailed regularly across the Atlantic Ocean to take advantage of the rich fishing grounds in Newfoundland (in modern Canada). However, the dense forests and harsh winters discouraged them from exploring more of North America. French explorers took up the challenge, searching for a new sea route to the Pacific and the riches of the East. Although they failed to find a northwest passage, they returned with valuable beaver furs, and also opened up the way for the French settlement of Canada. Meanwhile, from their bases in Mexico, the Spaniards explored the southern USA, drawn on by their dreams of gold.

MAP KEY

- ← Route of Panfilo de Narvaez and Álvar Núñez Cabeza de Vaca (1528–36)
- ← Route of Jacques Cartier (1534)
- ← Route of Jacques Cartier (1535–36)
- ← Route of Hernando de Soto and Luis de Moscoso (1539–43)
- ← Route of Coronado and Cárdenas (1540–42)
- ← Route of Samuel de Champlain (1604–07)
- ← Route of Samuel de Champlain (1608–16)
- ← Route of Robert de la Salle (1679–82)

◀ THE SPANISH IN FLORIDA

In 1528, Spanish conquistador Panfilo de Narvaez landed on the west coast of Florida and marched inland. After months of searching for gold, his men were forced back by native Americans (shown here). Continuing in five small boats, Narvaez sailed along the Gulf of Mexico, where he and four boats were lost. One survivor, Álvar Núñez Cabeza de Vaca, walked 2,000 km (1,240 miles) to Culiacán and finally into Mexico City.

◀ THE GREAT MISSISSIPPI

In 1539, another Spanish conquistador, Hernando de Soto, landed in Florida, with an army of 600 men and 200 horses, in search of gold. His brutal treatment of the native Americans led to fighting on his journey west to the Mississippi (shown in this painting). There was no gold, and de Soto died in 1542. His successor, Luis de Moscoso, took the surviving men home after a nightmare journey, chased to the coast by native Americans.

CARTIER IN NEW FRANCE ▶

A master navigator, Jacques Cartier was sent by King Francis I of France to find new lands. On his first expedition he found the St Lawrence River. On his second journey, using two native Americans as guides, he sailed up the St Lawrence, landing at Stadacona (modern Quebéc) and Hochelago (modern Montréal). His later attempt to found a colony there failed miserably.

◀ THE SCENIC ROUTE

Having failed to find cities of gold in Florida, the Spaniards set their sights on the southwest. In 1540, Francisco Vasquez de Coronado set out to find these cities, but failed. A member of his expedition, Garcia Lõpez de Cárdenas, went in search of the Colorado River, and became the first European to set eyes on the Grand Canyon.

DID YOU KNOW?

On his travels, Samuel de Champlain used men called *coureurs des bois* ("runners of the woods") as guides and interpreters. They were French fur trappers who went to Canada and lived with native Americans, learning their languages and customs.

◀ ALONG THE ST LAWRENCE

Although Cartier did not discover the northwest passage, the St Lawrence River became a major waterway for fishermen and fur traders. Then, in the early 1600s, Samuel de Champlain began a series of journeys that mapped the St Lawrence and explored the Great Lakes. This work took him 13 years. In 1608, he established a new trading post at Stadacona, which became the capital of New France.

VALUABLE TRADING AREAS ▶

Robert de la Salle went to North America in 1666 to seek his fortune from the fur trade. Then in 1679, he was instructed by Louis XIV to build forts across French territory. He travelled all the way to the Gulf of Mexico, where he claimed the land of the Mississippi Basin for France, naming it Louisiana after his king. La Salle was killed by his own men on his second expedition.

BEAVERS were trapped for their fur

Northeast Passage

DURING THE 16TH CENTURY, English and Dutch traders decided to search for a sea route that would take them along the far north of Russia to the riches of the East. They chose to sail in a northeasterly direction – a route that became known as the Northeast Passage. Many expeditions set off, backed by merchant companies, but it was a risky undertaking. Defeated by the desperate conditions, many were forced to turn back or met their death in the frozen seas. It was not until the late 19th century that a route along the treacherous coast of Siberian Russia was successfully navigated.

ARRIVAL IN RUSSIA ▶

In 1553, English navigator Richard Chancellor joined Sir Hugh Willoughby's expedition to find the Northeast Passage. Chancellor reached the White Sea, and continued across snow-covered land to Moscow. He was granted an audience with Tsar Ivan IV, who was happy to establish trade links with England.

RICHARD CHANCELLOR MEETS
THE TSAR IN HIS PALACE

MAP KEY

←	Voyage of Richard Chancellor (1553–54)
↙	Voyage of Sir Hugh Willoughby (1553)
←	Main voyage of Willem Barents (1596)
←	Voyage of Nils Nordenskjöld (1878–79)

COAT OF ARMS OF THE COMPANY OF
MERCHANT ADVENTURERS

◀ COAT OF ARMS

The expedition of 1553 was backed by the Company of Merchant Adventurers. Three ships set off, under the leadership of Sir Hugh Willoughby, with Richard Chancellor second in command. However, the ships became separated during a storm. Although Willoughby's ship reached Novaya Zemlya, it got trapped in ice on the way home and Willoughby and the crew all perished.

It was Finnish explorer Nils Nordenskjöld who finally navigated the full length of the Northeast Passage. He and a team of scientists sailed from Norway on the *Vega* in July 1878. Nordenskjöld headed east around the southern end of Novaya Zemlya and across the north of Siberia. Making good progress, he reached the mouth of the River Lena by August, but then got caught in thick fog and ice. Frozen in for winter, the *Vega* broke free of the ice in July 1879. Then Nordenskjöld rounded Cape Dezhnev and sailed through the Bering Strait into the Pacific Ocean.

SURVIVING THE COLD

utch navigator Willem Barents made three notable xpeditions to find the Northeast Passage. It was the hird voyage of 1596, however, that ended in disaster hen his ship got trapped in the ice. Forced to spend he winter on Novaya Zemlya, the men lived in a hut ade from the ship's timber. They kept a fire going, ut it was so cold that icicles formed on their beds. he survivors became the first Europeans to live rough an Arctic winter. Although the exploration as over, the men tried to get home in two small ats – Barents died, but his crew survived.

DID YOU KNOW?

The *Vega* had a specially strengthened wooden hull to withstand the pressure of the ice. It was originally built for whaling and seal hunting, and after the expedition was once again used for this purpose.

THE THREE VOYAGES OF BARENTS

arents was an experienced seaman who seemed an ideal person to find a ute to the East. In 1594, he reached Novaya Zemlya before being forced ack. He returned the following year, this time with seven ships, but the treacherous sea-ice made progress impossible and again he turned back. On the third voyage in 1596, with two ships, Barents sighted an ice-bound island, which he named Spitzbergen, meaning "jagged peaks". It was here, in the Svalbard archipelago, that the two ships were separated and Barents went on to his ill-fated end. Both the Barents Sea and Barents Island in Svalbard are named after him.

BREAKING THE ICE ▲

Today, the Northeast Passage is known as the Northern Sea Route. It is a busy commercial shipping lane, linking the Atlantic and Pacific Oceans across the far north of Russia. During winter, the seaway is covered in ice up to 2 m (7 ft) thick. Russian nuclear-powered icebreakers, like this one, are used to clear the ice to allow cargo ships and other vessels to pass through.

SPITZBERGEN is one of the ice-covered islands in the Svalbard archipelago

Northwest Passage

THE SEARCH FOR AN ALTERNATIVE SEA ROUTE to Asia challenged explorers for centuries. With the eastern route around Africa controlled by Portugal, and the western route around South America controlled by Spain, they turned their attention north. One possibility was to sail northwest around the top of North America, but as explorers soon discovered, that meant crossing some of the most treacherous seas in the world. Faced with appalling weather and icy conditions, English explorers led the search for what became known as the Northwest Passage. It was Norwegian explorer Roald Amundsen who finally sailed through in 1906.

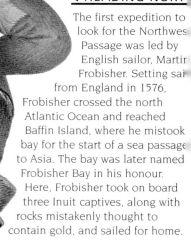

INUIT WOMAN and baby were taken to England by Frobisher in 1576

◀ HEADING NORTH

The first expedition to look for the Northwest Passage was led by English sailor, Martin Frobisher. Setting sail from England in 1576, Frobisher crossed the north Atlantic Ocean and reached Baffin Island, where he mistook bay for the start of a sea passage to Asia. The bay was later named Frobisher Bay in his honour. Here, Frobisher took on board three Inuit captives, along with rocks mistakenly thought to contain gold, and sailed for home.

Map labels:
ARCTIC OCEAN
Smith Sound
Jones Sound
Ellesmere Island
Lancaster Sound
Franklin Strait
Carey Islands
Greenland
Baffin Bay
Baffin Island
Gjoa Haven
Norwegian Sea
EUROPE
Oslo
Iceland
Shetland Islands
Davis Strait
Hudson Bay
Aberdeen
Frobisher Bay
London
Dartmouth
Nunap Isua
NORTH AMERICA
ATLANTIC OCEAN

MAP KEY

- ← Voyage of Martin Frobisher (1576)
- ← Voyage of John Davis (1585–87)
- ⇢ Voyage of Henry Hudson (1610–11)
- ← Voyage of William Baffin and Robert Bylot (1616)
- ← Voyage of Sir John Franklin (1845–47)
- ← Voyage of Roald Amundsen (1903–06)

IRON PYRITE ROCKS, KNOWN AS FOOLS' GOLD

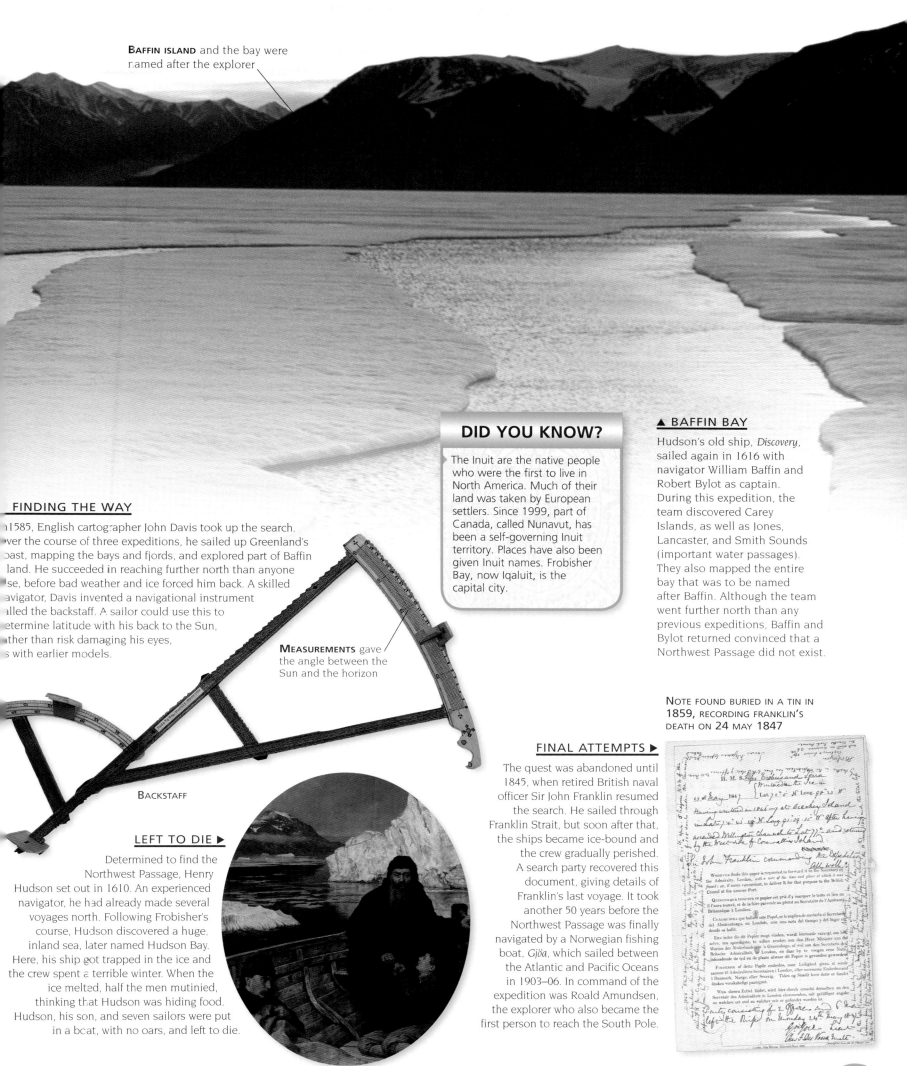

BAFFIN ISLAND and the bay were named after the explorer

DID YOU KNOW?

The Inuit are the native people who were the first to live in North America. Much of their land was taken by European settlers. Since 1999, part of Canada, called Nunavut, has been a self-governing Inuit territory. Places have also been given Inuit names. Frobisher Bay, now Iqaluit, is the capital city.

▲ BAFFIN BAY

Hudson's old ship, *Discovery*, sailed again in 1616 with navigator William Baffin and Robert Bylot as captain. During this expedition, the team discovered Carey Islands, as well as Jones, Lancaster, and Smith Sounds (important water passages). They also mapped the entire bay that was to be named after Baffin. Although the team went further north than any previous expeditions, Baffin and Bylot returned convinced that a Northwest Passage did not exist.

FINDING THE WAY

In 1585, English cartographer John Davis took up the search. Over the course of three expeditions, he sailed up Greenland's coast, mapping the bays and fjords, and explored part of Baffin Island. He succeeded in reaching further north than anyone else, before bad weather and ice forced him back. A skilled navigator, Davis invented a navigational instrument called the backstaff. A sailor could use this to determine latitude with his back to the Sun, rather than risk damaging his eyes, as with earlier models.

MEASUREMENTS gave the angle between the Sun and the horizon

BACKSTAFF

LEFT TO DIE ▶

Determined to find the Northwest Passage, Henry Hudson set out in 1610. An experienced navigator, he had already made several voyages north. Following Frobisher's course, Hudson discovered a huge, inland sea, later named Hudson Bay. Here, his ship got trapped in the ice and the crew spent a terrible winter. When the ice melted, half the men mutinied, thinking that Hudson was hiding food. Hudson, his son, and seven sailors were put in a boat, with no oars, and left to die.

NOTE FOUND BURIED IN A TIN IN 1859, RECORDING FRANKLIN'S DEATH ON 24 MAY 1847

FINAL ATTEMPTS ▶

The quest was abandoned until 1845, when retired British naval officer Sir John Franklin resumed the search. He sailed through Franklin Strait, but soon after that, the ships became ice-bound and the crew gradually perished. A search party recovered this document, giving details of Franklin's last voyage. It took another 50 years before the Northwest Passage was finally navigated by a Norwegian fishing boat, *Gjöa*, which sailed between the Atlantic and Pacific Oceans in 1903–06. In command of the expedition was Roald Amundsen, the explorer who also became the first person to reach the South Pole.

Pacific Pioneers

IN THE 16TH CENTURY, trade was still the driving force behind most voyages of exploration. The Portuguese and the Spaniards led the way – they were the first to reach the Spice Islands (the Moluccas), claiming them and the surrounding islands. Despite this, the Dutch established a base in the Spice Islands and explored the Pacific Ocean's trade routes. Other explorers set sail to find out if the legend of a huge southern continent was true. During their searches, many new islands were discovered.

▼ PRIZED SPICES

Nutmeg, cloves, and mace were three spices that grew only on the Spice Islands. Having at last occupied the Spice Islands and the East Indian islands, the Spaniards' next problem was to get the spices home by the quickest route. Andrés de Urdaneta believed it would be easiest to sail across the Pacific with them and became the first European to sail from west to east across the Pacific.

MAP KEY

◄— Voyage of Andrés de Urdaneta (1565)
◄— Voyage of Álvaro de Mendaña de Neira and Pedro de Gamboa (1567–69)
◄— Voyage of Álvaro de Mendaña de Neira and Pedro Fernandes de Quirós (1595–96)
—⌐— Voyage of Pedro Fernandes de Quirós (1605–06)
◄— Voyage of Luis Váez de Torres (1606–07)
◄— Voyage of Abel Tasman (1642–43)

DUTCH EAST INDIA COMPANY

In 1602, several rival groups of Dutc merchants joined together and forme the Dutch East India Company. From i headquarters at the port of Batavia (moder Jakarta), the company took control of th lucrative spice trade. The company's ship were sometimes blown off course on the way to Batavia, so the traders accidental ended up in unexplored water

PAINTING SHOWING DUTCH SETTLERS IN THE PORT OF BATAVIA ON THE ISLAND OF JAVA

LAGOON ON MAROVO ISLAND,
PART OF THE SOLOMON ISLANDS

ISLAND DISCOVERY ▲

Spanish explorer Álvaro de Mendaña de Neira set out from Callao, Peru, in 1567. Also on board was Spanish navigator Pedro de Gamboa. Their aim was to find the southern continent and convert the local people to Christianity. The voyage lasted almost two years, and covered 11,500 km (7,145 miles). They discovered the Solomon Islands, at first thought to be the tip of the southern continent. To take credit for discovering the islands, de Neira threw away Gamboa's maps and notes, and abandoned him in Mexico.

ASMAN'S TRAVELS ▶

nowledge of the South Pacific
ew with the voyages of Dutch
xplorer Abel Tasman. In
642, Tasman went in
earch of the mysterious
outhern continent. After
ailing east from Mauritius,
asman rounded the coast of
an Dieman's Land, later
enamed Tasmania after him.
ontinuing east, he discovered
ew Zealand before heading
orth to Tonga and Fiji. He
iled, however, to find Australia.

DISASTROUS JOURNEY ▶

Álvaro de Mendaña de Neira's voyage
of 1595 was meant to set up a colony
in the Solomon Islands. The trip
ended in disaster when islanders
were slaughtered, de Neira died,
and the Spaniards fought among
themselves. The Portuguese
navigator Pedro Fernandes de
Quirós took the survivors home.
In 1605, he sailed again, visiting
the Cook Islands and Vanuatu
(New Hebrides). When his ship
became separated from the
expedition, it fell to Luis Váez de
Torres to take command a year
later. He did not find the southern
continent but sailed around New
Guinea, proving that it was an island.

DID YOU KNOW?

The remote Easter Island lies
in the Pacific Ocean 3,600 km
(2,200 miles) off the coast of
Chile. The first European to see
the island was Dutch explorer,
Jacob Roggeveen, in 1722.
He found it on Easter Day
and named it "Isla de Pascua"
("Easter Island" in Spanish).

ISLANDERS FROM PAPUA NEW GUINEA
DRESSED IN TRADITIONAL COSTUME

Science and Discovery

FROM THE 18TH CENTURY ONWARDS, there was a change in the nature of exploration. With most of the world now discovered by European explorers, trade and conquest were no longer the sole motives for journeys. The new explorers were scientists, driven by scientific curiosity to undertake some of the most daring expeditions of all. Some sent back specimens of plants and animals unknown in Europe. Others filled in the gaps remaining on the maps. Today, scientific discovery continues to unlock the secrets of planet Earth. With better technology and transport, modern explorers have even been able to investigate the depths of the oceans and probe the planets in our solar system.

58–59 RUSSIAN EXPLORATION

In the 1700s, Tsar Peter the Great sent out explorers to Siberia. He wanted to bring the region under Russian control, and discover if Asia and North America were linked.

60–61 CAPTAIN COOK

Between 1768 and 1779, Cook mapped the coasts of Tahiti, Australia, and New Zealand, and discovered the islands of Hawaii.

Replica of Cook's famous ship, the *Endeavour*.

62–63 ACROSS A CONTINENT

By the late 1700s, large parts of North America had been mapped and explored. Now the race was on to cross the continent from coast to coast.

64–65 NATURALIST EXPLORERS

During the 18th century, scientists began to accompany expeditions, curious to find out more about the world and wildlife.

The Galapagos Islands were explored by Darwin in 1835.

66–67 EXPLORING AFRICA

One of the greatest challenges for explorers in Africa was to locate the source, length, and routes of its great rivers.

68–69 AFRICAN ADVENTURES

Exploring Africa's interior and bringing Christianity to its peoples inspired David Livingstone and those who followed him.

This painting shows the first meeting between Henry Morton Stanley and David Livingstone.

70–71 ACROSS AUSTRALIA

At first, European settlement in Australia was confined to the coast. From the early 1800s, however, explorers investigated the centre of the continent and eventually crossed it from south to north.

72–73 EXPLORING ARABIA

The harsh conditions of Arabia did not deter European explorers as they attempted to cross the deserts and enter cities forbidden to them.

Richard Burton's accounts of his travels in Arabia were recorded in his book.

74–75 CONQUERING THE NORTH POLE

Scientific enquiry, combined with the a desire to be the first there, drove men across the frozen Arctic Ocean to the North Pole.

Antarctica is the coldest place on Earth.

76–77 RACE TO THE SOUTH POLE

Scientific exploration of Antarctica did not begin until the 1890s.

78–79 OCEAN EXPLORATION

The modern exploration of the oceans began in the mid-19th century, with the benefits of advanced technology. But even today, vast areas of the seabed remain unexplored.

80–81 ON TOP OF THE WORLD

Mountain peaks offer not only a scientific challenge but also a physical challenge of being the first to the top.

Tenzing Norgay and Edmund Hillary take a rest on Mount Everest.

82–83 RACE TO THE MOON

Neil Armstrong became the first person to set foot on the Moon in 1969. The long-held dream of exploring space had become a reality.

84–85 EXPLORING THE PLANETS

As rocket technology has improved, scientist can send out unmanned space vehicles on long-term missions to explore other planets.

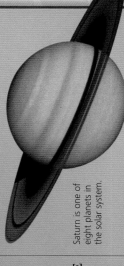
Saturn is one of eight planets in the solar system.

LAGOON ON MAROVO ISLAND,
PART OF THE SOLOMON ISLANDS

ISLAND DISCOVERY ▲

Spanish explorer Álvaro de Mendaña de Neira set out from Callao, Peru, in 1567. Also on board was Spanish navigator Pedro de Gamboa. Their aim was to find the southern continent and convert the local people to Christianity. The voyage lasted almost two years, and covered 11,500 km (7,145 miles). They discovered the Solomon Islands, at first thought to be the tip of the southern continent. To take credit for discovering the islands, de Neira threw away Gamboa's maps and notes, and abandoned him in Mexico.

ASMAN'S TRAVELS ▶

nowledge of the South Pacific
rew with the voyages of Dutch
xplorer Abel Tasman. In
642, Tasman went in
earch of the mysterious
outhern continent. After
ailing east from Mauritius,
asman rounded the coast of
an Dieman's Land, later
enamed Tasmania after him.
ontinuing east, he discovered
ew Zealand before heading
orth to Tonga and Fiji. He
iled, however, to find Australia.

DISASTROUS JOURNEY ▶

Álvaro de Mendaña de Neira's voyage
of 1595 was meant to set up a colony
in the Solomon Islands. The trip
ended in disaster when islanders
were slaughtered, de Neira died,
and the Spaniards fought among
themselves. The Portuguese
navigator Pedro Fernandes de
Quirós took the survivors home.
In 1605, he sailed again, visiting
the Cook Islands and Vanuatu
(New Hebrides). When his ship
became separated from the
expedition, it fell to Luis Váez de
Torres to take command a year
later. He did not find the southern
continent but sailed around New
Guinea, proving that it was an island.

ISLANDERS FROM PAPUA NEW GUINEA
DRESSED IN TRADITIONAL COSTUME

DID YOU KNOW?

The remote Easter Island lies
in the Pacific Ocean 3,600 km
(2,200 miles) off the coast of
Chile. The first European to see
the island was Dutch explorer,
Jacob Roggeveen, in 1722.
He found it on Easter Day
and named it "Isla de Pascua"
("Easter Island" in Spanish).

Science and Discovery

FROM THE 18TH CENTURY ONWARDS, there was a change in the nature of exploration. With most of the world now discovered by European explorers, trade and conquest were no longer the sole motives for journeys. The new explorers were scientists, driven by scientific curiosity to undertake some of the most daring expeditions of all. Some sent back specimens of plants and animals unknown in Europe. Others filled in the gaps remaining on the maps. Today, scientific discovery continues to unlock the secrets of planet Earth. With better technology and transport, modern explorers have even been able to investigate the depths of the oceans and probe the planets in our solar system.

58–59 RUSSIAN EXPLORATION

In the 1700s, Tsar Peter the Great sent out explorers to Siberia. He wanted to bring the region under Russian control, and discover if Asia and North America were linked.

60–61 CAPTAIN COOK

Between 1768 and 1779, Cook mapped the coasts of Tahiti, Australia, and New Zealand, and discovered the islands of Hawaii.

Replica of Cook's famous ship, the *Endeavour*.

62–63 ACROSS A CONTINENT

By the late 1700s, large parts of North America had been mapped and explored. Now the race was on to cross the continent from coast to coast.

64–65 NATURALIST EXPLORERS

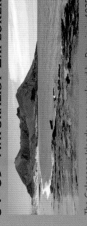

The Galapagos Islands were explored by Darwin in 1835.

During the 18th century, scientists began to accompany expeditions, curious to find out more about the world and wildlife.

66–67 EXPLORING AFRICA

One of the greatest challenges for explorers in Africa was to locate the source, length, and routes of its great rivers.

68–69 AFRICAN ADVENTURES

Exploring Africa's interior and bringing Christianity to its peoples inspired David Livingstone and those who followed him.

This painting shows the first meeting between Henry Morton Stanley and David Livingstone.

70–71 ACROSS AUSTRALIA

At first, European settlement in Australia was confined to the coast. From the early 1800s, however, explorers investigated the centre of the continent and eventually crossed it from south to north.

72–73 EXPLORING ARABIA

The harsh conditions of Arabia did not deter European explorers as they attempted to cross the deserts and enter cities forbidden to them.

Richard Burton's accounts of his travels in Arabia were recorded in his book.

74–75 CONQUERING THE NORTH POLE

Scientific enquiry, combined with the a desire to be the first there, drove men across the frozen Arctic Ocean to the North Pole.

76–77 RACE TO THE SOUTH POLE

Antarctica is the coldest place on Earth.

Scientific exploration of Antarctica did not begin until the 1890s.

78–79 OCEAN EXPLORATION

The modern exploration of the oceans began in the mid-19th century, with the benefits of advanced technology. But even today, vast areas of the seabed remain unexplored.

80–81 ON TOP OF THE WORLD

Mountain peaks offer not only a scientific challenge but also a physical challenge of being the first to the top.

Tenzing Norgay and Edmund Hillary take a rest on Mount Everest.

82–83 RACE TO THE MOON

Neil Armstrong became the first person to set foot on the Moon in 1969. The long-held dream of exploring space had become a reality.

84–85 EXPLORING THE PLANETS

As rocket technology has improved, scientist can send out unmanned space vehicles on long-term missions to explore other planets.

Saturn is one of eight planets in the solar system.

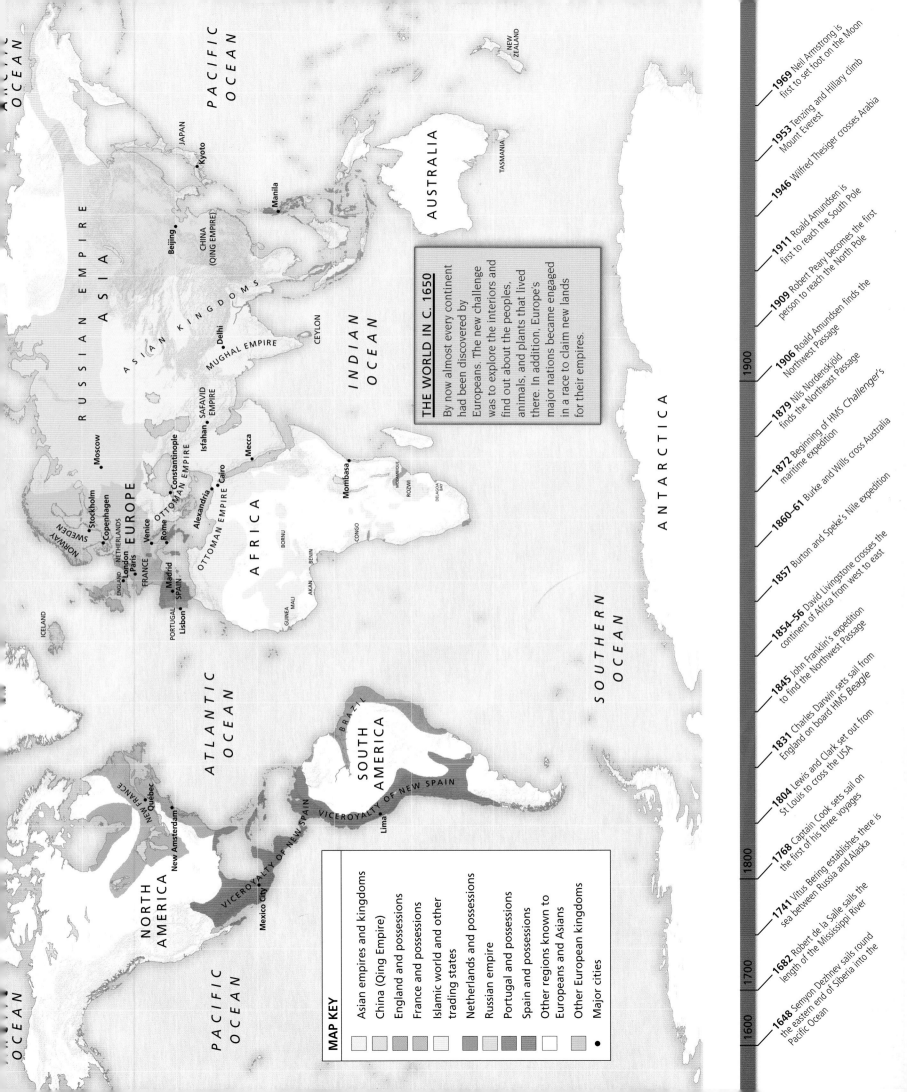

ARCTIC OCEAN

PACIFIC OCEAN

JAPAN
Kyoto

ASIA

RUSSIAN EMPIRE

CHINA (QING EMPIRE)
Beijing
Manila

ASIAN KINGDOMS

MUGHAL EMPIRE
Delhi
CEYLON

INDIAN OCEAN

AUSTRALIA

TASMANIA

NEW ZEALAND

Moscow

EUROPE
Stockholm
SWEDEN
Copenhagen
NETHERLANDS
London
Paris
ENGLAND
FRANCE
Venice
Rome
Madrid
SPAIN
PORTUGAL
Lisbon

NORWAY

ICELAND

OTTOMAN EMPIRE
Constantinople
Istahan
SAFAVID EMPIRE

Alexandria
OTTOMAN EMPIRE
Cairo
Mecca

AFRICA

BORNU
BENIN
CONGO
GUINEA
MALI
AKAN

Mombasa
MOZAMBIQUE
ROZWI
DELAGOA BAY

ANTARCTICA

THE WORLD IN C. 1650

By now almost every continent had been discovered by Europeans. The new challenge was to explore the interiors and find out about the peoples, animals, and plants that lived there. In addition, Europe's major nations became engaged in a race to claim new lands for their empires.

NORTH AMERICA

NEW FRANCE
Québec
New Amsterdam

Mexico City
VICEROYALTY OF NEW SPAIN

ATLANTIC OCEAN

BRAZIL
SOUTH AMERICA
VICEROYALTY OF NEW SPAIN
Lima

PACIFIC OCEAN

SOUTHERN OCEAN

MAP KEY

- Asian empires and kingdoms
- China (Qing Empire)
- England and possessions
- France and possessions
- Islamic world and other trading states
- Netherlands and possessions
- Russian empire
- Portugal and possessions
- Spain and possessions
- Other regions known to Europeans and Asians
- Other European kingdoms
- Major cities

Cape Dezhnev, the northeastern tip of Russia, is named after Russian explorer and government agent, Semyon Dezhnev. In 1648, he is thought to have sailed around the cape, and may have discovered the Bering Strait nearly a century before Bering himself. Dezhnev's journey was even more remarkable because it was made in a small, flat-bottomed boat, called a koch

Russian Exploration

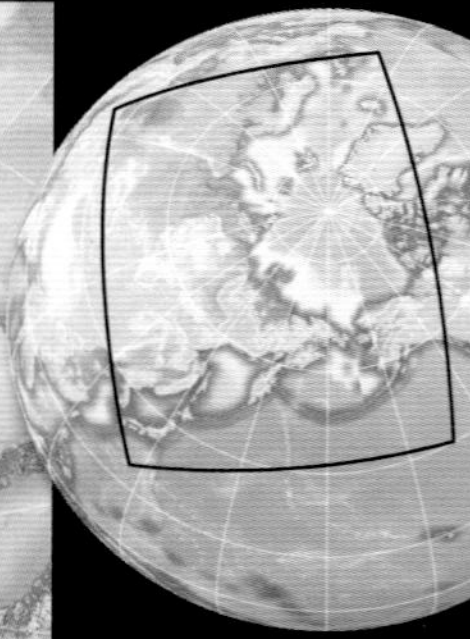

ALTHOUGH RECORDS ARE SCARCE, the Russian tsars began sending explorers into Siberia from the late 16th century onwards. Most notable among these were Semyon Dezhnev and Vitus Bering. In the early 1700s, Tsar Peter the Great decided to bring Siberia under Russian control. He wanted to expand trade, establish useful ports, and discover whether Asia and North America were joined together by a land bridge. In 1725, he appointed Vitus Bering, a Danish officer in the Russian navy, to explore Asia's east coast. Bering was convinced that the two continents were separated by water but failed to prove it on his first expedition. In 1733, Bering organized the Great Northern Expedition – a larger, more ambitious voyage to map the north coast of Siberia. Then in 1741, he set out once again to prove that water separates Asia and North America.

Map labels: Moscow, Ural Mountains, Archangel, Yekaterinburg, Barents Sea, Kara Sea, Greenland, Yeniseysk, ASIA, Siberia, ARCTIC OCEAN, Laptev Sea, Yakutsk, East Siberian Sea, Bering Strait, Okhotsk, Cape Dezhnev, NORTH AMERICA, Alaska, Sea of Okhotsk, St Lawrence Island, Bering Sea, Petropavlovsk-Kamchatskiy, Bering Island, PACIFIC OCEAN

MAP KEY

- Route of Semyon Dezhnev (1648)
- First route of Vitus Bering (1725–30)
- Route of Great Northern Expedition (1733–42)
- Second route of Vitus Bering (1741–42)

◄ RECORDING WILDLIFE

Following the failure of his first expedition to establish that water separated Siberia and Alaska, Vitus Bering embarked on a second attempt in 1741. Also on board was naturalist Georg Steller, studying and recording the wildlife, such as the sea lions. The voyage succeeded in its aim, but many men died, including Bering. Steller, however, was one of the few survivors.

DID YOU KNOW?

▸ Due to Bering's expeditions, Alaska became Russian territory. In 1867, however, the USA bought Alaska from Russia for $7,200,000. Later explorations revealed deposits of gold and oil.

MAMMOTH REMAINS ▸

The Great Northern Expedition across Russia's northern coast was through land so close to the Arctic Circle that the ground was permanently frozen. Explorers succeeded in mapping the entire length of coastline, though it took them much longer than expected. It was here that explorers also made amazing discoveries – they found the remains of woolly mammoths, which lived from about 5 million to 10,000 years ago.

◄ HIDDEN RICHES

Once considered a vast wasteland, Siberia is now one of Russia's most valuable resources. The region is rich in minerals and metals, with some of the world's largest deposits of diamonds, gold, nickel, silver, and zinc. These were first discovered in the 18th century, but large-scale exploitation took place during the 20th century, opening up a new chapter in Russian exploration.

WOOLLY MAMMOTH

◄ PRZEWALSKI'S TRAVELS

In the 19th century, Russian explorer and naturalist Nikolai Przewalski travelled widely throughout Central Asia, exploring this remote region and collecting specimens of plants and animals. He discovered the only surviving species of wild horse, which was later named after him.

Captain Cook

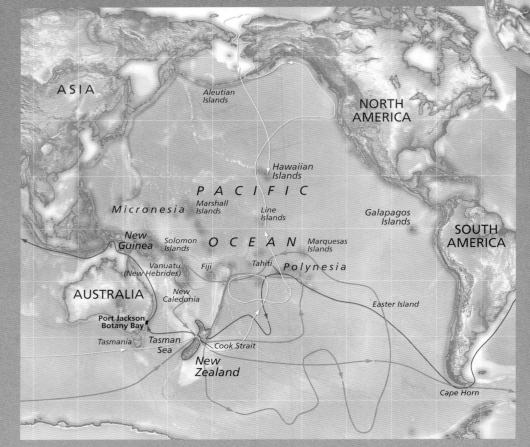

ASIA

Aleutian
Islands

NORTH
AMERICA

Hawaiian
Islands

P A C I F I C

Micronesia   Marshall
Islands   Line
Islands   Galapagos
Islands

New
Guinea   Solomon   O C E A N   Marquesas
Islands   Islands   SOUTH
AMERICA

Vanuatu   Fiji   Tahiti   P o l y n e s i a
(New Hebrides)

AUSTRALIA   New
Caledonia

Port Jackson
Botany Bay   Easter Island

Tasmania   Tasman   Cook Strait
Sea

New
Zealand

Cape Horn

MAP KEY

← First voyage of James Cook
(1768–71)

Second voyage of James Cook
(1772–75)

← Third voyage of James Cook
(1776–79)

UNTIL THE MIDDLE OF THE 18TH CENTURY, very little was known in Europe about the south Pacific. Many people believed that there was a large land mass there – a southern continent. In 1768, English explorer and navigator Captain James Cook set out to find out more about this legendary continent. Scientists and artists accompanied his three voyages. Cook charted vast tracts of the Pacific, discovered several islands, and brought home detailed information on the places he visited.

DID YOU KNOW?

In the 18th century, scurvy killed more sailors than all other causes, and at the time no one was sure what caused it. On *Endeavour*, Cook changed the sailors' diet, introducing items rich in vitamin C to ward off scurvy. It was so effective, others adopted the practice.

ENDEAVOUR ▶

For his first voyage, Cook chose a ship originally built to carry coal around Britain. The ship was refitted and renamed *Endeavour*. There was room for a crew of 93 men, including a team of scientists led by the naturalist Joseph Banks, and the ship's artist Sydney Parkinson. Shown here is a replica of the *Endeavour* .

◀ FIRST VOYAGE

On 26 August 1768, Cook sailed to the island of Tahiti. There, he spent three months observing the planet Venus as it passed between the Earth and the Sun – the official reason for the voyage. But Cook also had secret instructions from the British government to find the fabled southern continent. Heading south, Cook charted the coasts of New Zealand and eastern Australia. He had proved that New Zealand and Australia were not linked to a southern continent. In the meantime, the ship's artist Sydney Parkinson recorded everything he saw – plants, animals, and the local Maori people.

PORTRAIT
OF A MAORI BY
SYDNEY PARKINSON

ANTARCTIC ADVENTURE ▶

In 1772, Cook was sent on a second voyage to learn more about the southern continent. Sailing further south into the Southern Ocean, his two ships, *Resolution* and *Adventure*, became the first ever to cross the Antarctic Circle before fog and ice forced them to turn back. Although Cook never saw Antarctica, he correctly concluded that Antarctica was the southern continent.

◀ HAWAIIAN TRAGEDY

Cook's third and final voyage in 1776 took him north in search of the elusive Northwest Passage. On the way, he discovered the islands of Hawaii, which he named the Sandwich Islands. From Hawaii, Cook sailed east to the Canadian coast, then north towards the Bering Strait. With no passage in sight, he returned to Hawaii for the winter, where he was killed on 14 February 1779, in a skirmish about a stolen boat.

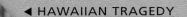

MODERN HAWAIIAN
ISLANDER – traditions
and ceremonies are still
re-enacted on the islands

Alex Mackenzie
From Canada
by land
22d July 1793

◄ WATERY ROUT[E]

The name of Scottish explor[er] Alexander Mackenzie remai[ns] inscribed on a rock in Briti[sh] Columbia. He had passe[d] this spot in 1793 during [a] mission to find a waterw[ay] to the Pacific Ocean. A[n] earlier effort had faile[d] but this second attem[pt] succeeded when h[e] followed the Pea[ce] River to the coas[t]

Across a Continent

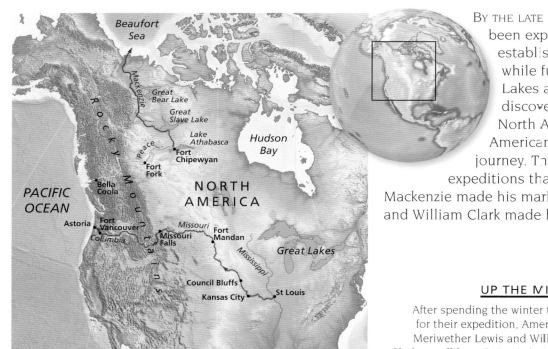

Beaufort Sea

Mackenzie
Rocky Mountains
Peace
Great Bear Lake
Great Slave Lake
Lake Athabasca
Fort Chipewyan
Fort Fork
Bella Coola
Hudson Bay

PACIFIC OCEAN

NORTH AMERICA

Astoria
Fort Vancouver
Columbia
Missouri
Missouri Falls
Fort Mandan
Great Lakes
Mississippi
Council Bluffs
Kansas City
St Louis

BY THE LATE 18TH CENTURY, only parts of North America had been explored and mapped. English settlers had established colonies along the continent's east coast, while further north, the French had explored the Great Lakes and reached the Mississippi River. Despite these discoveries, no European explorer had ever crossed North America, and it is unlikely that any native Americans would have attempted such an enormous journey. The breakthrough came with two legendary expeditions that opened up the continent. Alexander Mackenzie made his mark in Canada before Meriwether Lewis and William Clark made history in the USA.

MAP KEY

← First route of Alexander Mackenzie (1789)
← Second route of Alexander Mackenzie (1792–93)
← Route of Meriwether Lewis and William Clark (1804–06)

UP THE MISSOURI ►

After spending the winter training for their expedition, Americans Meriwether Lewis and William Clark set off from St Louis in May 1804. On board their three boats were 43 soldiers and supplies. As they sailed up the Missouri River, the explorers established relations and exchanged gifts with the native American tribes living nearby.

Lewis and Clark

In 1803, American President Thomas Jefferson chose two men to lead an expedition to Louisiana, a vast region recently acquired from the French. Their mission was to find a route from the Mississippi River to the Pacific coast. The two men were Jefferson's private secretary, Meriwether Lewis, and his friend, William Clark. The pair had met in the army, where Lewis was a captain. After their successful mission, both men were rewarded. Lewis was appointed Governor of Louisiana and Clark was made Governor of Missouri.

MERIWETHER LEWIS

WILLIAM CLARK

SACAJAWEA became a valuable member of Lewis and Clark's expedition

FORT MANDAN ▲

In November 1804, the party stopped in the land of the Mandan Indians and built a log fort for the winter. During their stay, they met a French hunter, Toussaint Charbonneau, and his wife, a local woman named Sacajawea. The couple joined the expedition as interpreters and helped guide Lewis and Clark through the treacherous Rocky Mountains.

◀ CROSSING THE ROCKIES

Leaving Fort Mandan in April 1805, Lewis and Clark's group headed west up the Missouri. At the Missouri Falls, they built makeshift carts so they could haul their boats round the dangerous rapids at the base of the waterfalls. A worse ordeal awaited them when they had to cross the Rocky Mountains on horseback. Their courage was rewarded in November 1805. Paddling down the Columbia River, they finally reached the Pacific coast.

◀ JOURNEY HOME

Lewis and Clark began the long journey back home in March 1806. They reached St Louis in September, having covered more than 12,000 km (7,450 miles), much of it through unknown territory. Although their route to the Pacific was not practical, their expedition had proved a great success. Their journals were packed with details and drawings of the remarkable places, plants, and animals they had seen.

Naturalist Explorers

A NEW TYPE OF EXPLORER began to emerge during the 18th century. These explorers were scientists, eager to travel and learn more about the world through study and research. Scientific expeditions were now sponsored by learned societies and governments, with teams of scholars involved. Rather than fame and fortune, these travellers were driven by the quest for knowledge and scientific discovery. The perfect place to start their search was in the rainforests of South America, home to more than one-third of all plant and animal life on Earth.

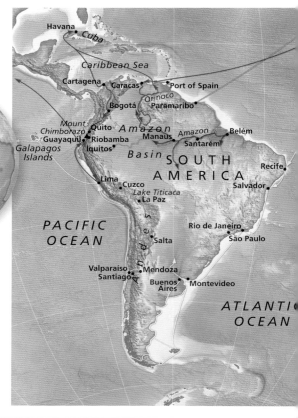

▲ AMAZON EXPEDITION

The French Academy of Sciences sent the gifted mathematician Charles-Marie de la Condamine to South America in 1735 as part of a geographical investigation concerning the shape of the Earth. Once this research was finished, la Condamine explored the Amazon. In the process, he found that rubber is made from the sap of rubber trees, and was the first scientist to follow the course of the River Amazon.

▲ PLANT LIFE

The German naturalist Alexander von Humboldt spent five years in South America from 1799. With French botanist, Aimé Bonpland, he sailed down the Orinoco River, and climbed Mount Chimborazo in the Andes. The two men, shown above, collected a huge amount of scientific data, including more than 3,000 new species of plants.

MAP KEY

➤ Route of Charles-Marie de la Condamine (1735–45)
➤ Route of Alexander von Humboldt (1799–1804)
➤ Route of Charles Darwin (1831–36)
➤ Route of Alfred Wallace and Henry Bates (1848–59)

VOLCANIC GALAPAGOS ISLANDS

◀ RAINFOREST INSECTS

Inspired by the writings of Alexander von Humboldt, the British naturalists Alfred Wallace and Henry Bates set off for the Amazon rainforest in 1848. Bates collected more than 14,000 species of insects, with half of them unknown to European scientists. Poor health forced Bates to leave South America after 11 years of study. Wallace was also an avid collector, but lost all of his specimens when the ship carrying him back to England caught fire and sank in 1852.

PAGES FROM BATES'S NOTEBOOKS SHOWING SOME OF THE INSECTS HE FOUND

Charles Darwin

Born into a wealthy English family, Charles Darwin (1809–1882) studied medicine and theology at university. However, he abandoned both to pursue his interest in natural history. In 1831, at the age of 23, Darwin was offered the post of naturalist on board HMS *Beagle*. During the five-year voyage to South America, Darwin collected evidence that would lead him to his theory of how life on Earth evolved.

MEGATHERIUM stood about 7 m (23 ft) tall and weighed the same as an elephant

FOSSILIZED BONES OF *MEGATHERIUM*

▼ VOYAGE OF THE *BEAGLE*

HMS *Beagle* set sail from England in December 1831 and headed across the Atlantic Ocean to South America. The crew spent more than three years surveying and charting the coastline, while Darwin spent much of the time exploring the land. He collected fossils and specimens of animals and plants, before writing down their details in his cramped cabin. The ship reached the Galapagos Islands in September 1835, where Darwin made many discoveries because of the area's unique wildlife.

▲ FOSSIL FINDINGS

In South America, Charles Darwin excavated the fossilized bones of extinct animals. He recognized *Megatherium* as a giant ground sloth with similarities to modern tree-living sloths. This discovery helped to convince Darwin that animals change gradually over time to suit their environment. It formed the basis of his theory of evolution, which changed the course of science.

THEORY OF EVOLUTION ▶

On the Galapagos Islands, Darwin noticed that birds had different beaks depending on where they lived. On one island, finches had beaks suited to catching insects, while on another, the beaks were ideal for feeding on flowers and fruit. It was clear that these birds had evolved beaks to suit the types of food that were available. This gave Darwin the ground-breaking idea that species adapted in order to survive.

Exploring Africa

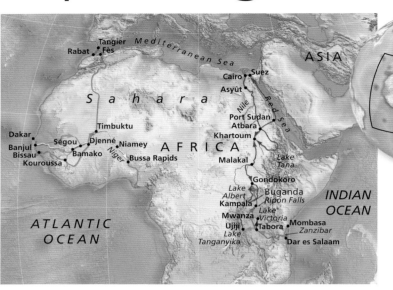

MAP KEY

- ⬅ Route of Mungo Park (1795–97)
- ⬅ Route of Mungo Park (1805–06)
- ⬅ Route of René Caillié (1827–28)
- ⬅ Route of Richard Burton and John Speke (1857–58)
- ⬅ Route of John Speke (1858)
- ⬅ Route of John Speke and James Grant (1860–63)
- ⬅ Route of Samuel Baker (1861–65)

ALTHOUGH PORTUGUESE EXPLORERS had sailed around Afri to reach Asia from the late 15th century, Europeans knew very little about the continent, other than th ports they visited along the coast. The vast interi of Africa remained a mystery – even though powerful empires had flourished there for hundreds of years. This changed in 1788, when British botanist Joseph Banks founded the African Association in London. The Association agreed to sponsor several expeditions to discover more about nort and west Africa, and to search for the source of the River Nile.

MUNGO FARK SETS OFF ▶

The African Association chose Scottish doctor Mungo Park to explore the River Niger (right) in West Africa. Park reached the Niger at Ségou (in modern Mali) in July 1796. He returned to Africa in 1805 to trace the river to its source, but the expedition was a disaster. Park drowned at the Bussa Rapids when his canoe was ambushed by hostile tribesmen.

◀ ACROSS THE SAHAR

In 1824, the Geographical Society of Paris offere a prize to the first explorer to reach Timbuktu i the Sahara Desert, and come back alive. Thre years later, a young Frenchman, René Caillié set out on the long and risky journe Disguised as an Arab (to avoid drawin attention to himself), Caillié reache Timbuktu in April 1828. He wa disappointed to find mud hut: instead of a city paved with gold

ARRIVAL AT LAKE TANGANYIKA ▶

By the time he set out for Africa, British explorer Richard Burton was already a seasoned traveller. His companion, John Speke, had recently left the army and was eager to explore Africa. The two men left Zanzibar in June 1857, and headed west to Lake Tanganyika where Burton fell seriously ill. Continuing alone, Speke discovered another large lake, which he named Lake Victoria. He was convinced, correctly, that this was the source of the Nile, but Burton disagreed. He claimed that the source was Lake Tanganyika.

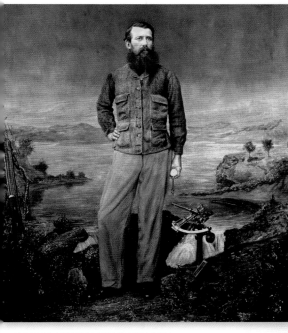

SPEKE SEEKS THE TRUTH

To settle the argument, Speke returned to Africa in 1860 with James Grant. They travelled up the west coast of Lake Victoria and became the first Europeans to visit the kingdom of Buganda (part of modern Uganda). Speke continued to the northern end of the lake where, in 1862, he found the source of the Nile at Ripon Falls.

THE BAKERS JOIN THE SEARCH

Larger-than-life explorer Samuel Baker and his wife Florence set off to search for the source of the Nile. They also hoped to meet up with Speke and Grant. When they met the explorers in Gondokora (Sudan), they heard the news that Speke had found the source of the Nile. Not deterred, the Bakers set off to explore another great lake to the west, which they reached in March 1864. They named it Lake Albert.

DID YOU KNOW?

Without the help of African people, early European expeditions would have been impossible. Some were hired to carry food and equipment, while others worked as interpreters and negotiators. About 350 men were needed for a large expedition. Many died on the journey.

African Adventures

EUROPEANS UNDERTOOK LONG AND DIFFICULT expeditions to explore Africa in the 19th century. These journeys often followed the great African rivers that took men into the heart of the continent. Among the most famous explorers of this time were David Livingstone and Henry Morton Stanley. Livingstone first went to Africa to try to improve life for the Africans, while Henry Morton Stanley was sent there to search for Livingstone. Both explorers faced continual danger from wild animals, sickness, and the tough terrain.

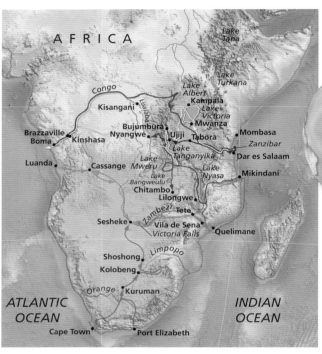

MAP KEY

- ← Route of David Livingstone (1841–52)
- ← Route of David Livingstone (1854–56)
- ← Route of David Livingstone (1858–64)
- ← Route of David Livingstone (1866–73)
- ← Route of Henry Morton Stanley (1871–72)
- ← Route of Henry Morton Stanley (1874–77)
- ← Route of Henry Morton Stanley (1887–89)

EXPLORING THE ZAMBEZI ▶

On his first trip to Africa in 1841, Livingstone reached the Zambezi River. Between 1854 and 1856, Livingstone crossed the African continent from west to east, and followed the Zambezi to the sea. Backed by the Royal Geographical Society, his aim was to open up the Zambezi as a highway into Africa. On the way, he visited a great waterfall, which he named Victoria Falls, after Queen Victoria. In 1858, Livingstone returned to explore the Zambezi again, but was prevented from getting any further by the raging rapids.

David Livingstone

Born in England into a religious family, David Livingstone (1813–73) qualified as a doctor and joined the London Missionary Society. He spent most of his adult life in Africa.

◀ SOURCE OF THE NILE

Once he was back in England, Livingstone began planning to fulfil a lifelong dream – to discover the source of the Nile, believing that this had not yet been accomplished. Although he was now in his fifties, he set off again in 1866, centring his search to the north of Lake Tanganyika. Livingstone discovered several lakes but was held back by his failing health. Exhausted and sick, he was carried to Ujiji (shown here) to recuperate in October 1871. Meanwhile, people back home began to fear he was dead.

◀ A FAMOUS MEETING

In 1871, the *New York Herald* newspaper sent reporter Henry Morton Stanley to search for Livingstone. After a long trek, Stanley reached Ujiji where he found the explorer and greeted him with the famous words "Dr Livingstone, I presume?". Although ill, Livingstone set off for the Lualaba River, convinced that it was the real route to the source of the Nile. He died in 1873 on the shore of Lake Bangweulu.

STANLEY IN THE CONGO ▶

After Livingstone's death, Stanley returned to Africa in 1874 to explore the River Congo. His boat, the *Lady Alice*, was specially built for the expedition. It could be dismantled and carried in sections around rapids and over obstacles. Stanley headed for Lake Tanganyika, then to the Lualaba River, which he proved was part of the Congo. Skirting the Stanley Falls, he embarked on the perilous 1,600-km (992-mile) journey down the Congo to its mouth at Boma. His expedition took three years and cost more than 200 lives.

Across Australia

CAPTAIN COOK'S EXPLORATION of southeast Australia led the way for the founding of the first British colonies. The settlers were mostly convicts, sent to Australia instead of prison in the late 1700s, but others soon followed. Most of Australia, however, remained a mystery. The settlers stayed near the coast, so very little was known about the continent. As numbers increased, so did the need for more grazing land. The race was now on to learn more about the interior and find routes across Australia.

◀ LAKE EYRE

Edward Eyre emigrated to Australia from Britain in 1833. Before turning to exploration, he worked as an overlander (driving cattle across country). In 1839–40, he explored the area north of Adelaide to Lake Eyre, which was named after him. The following year, Eyre went on to lead an expedition across the south of Australia, from Adelaide to Albany.

MAP KEY

← Route of Edward Eyre (1839-40)
← Route of Edward Eyre (1841)
← Route of Robert Burke and William Wills (1860-61)
← Route of John McDouall Stuart (1860)
← Route of John McDouall Stuart (1861)
← Route of John McDouall Stuart (1862)

◀ BURKE AND WILLS

In 1859, the government of South Australia offered a prize to the first person to cross Australia from south to north. The first expedition to do so was led by former soldier Robert Burke and surveyor William Wills. It was the largest and most expensive expedition ever organized in Australia. Burke and Wills left Melbourne on 20 August 1860, cheered on by the crowds who came to see them off.

GULF OF CARPENTARIA ▲

By October 1860, Burke and Wills had reached the town of Menindee. From there, they headed towards Cooper's Creek, where the party split up. With supplies for three months, Burke, Wills, John King, and Charles Gray set off north. It was a tough journey through the desert, with blistering heat and choking sandstorms. But in February 1861, they finally reached tidal waters near the Gulf of Carpentaria, and realized that they were near the sea.

STATUE OF JOHN MCDOUALL STUART

DEATH AT COOPER'S CREEK

y now, most of their food had gone and their health was ailing. Gray died in April 1861. The other three men made their ainful way back to Cooper's Creek. To their horror, they found hat the support party they had left behind had headed home a ew hours earlier. Burke and Wills died from starvation. Months ater, a rescue party found King, the only survivor, who had been ving with a group of local Aboriginal people.

DID YOU KNOW?

The Aboriginal people had lived in Australia for tens of thousands of years before Europeans arrived. They were skilled at surviving in the harsh conditions.

JOHN MCDOUALL STUART ▶

Already an experienced traveller, John McDouall Stuart set out from Adelaide in March 1860 to cross Australia. On his first two attempts, Stuart reached the centre of the continent but was forced to turn back. His third journey was a success. Stuart left Adelaide in October 1861, and reached the sea near modern-day Darwin the following July. He did not realize, however, that his rivals, Burke and Wills, had already crossed the continent by a different route.

Exploring Arabia

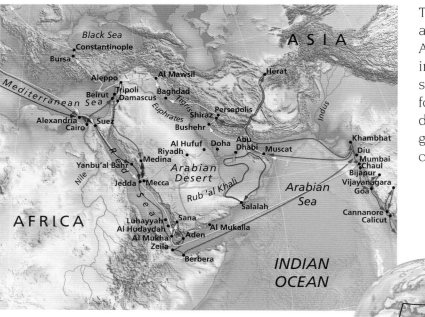

THE DESERTS OF ARABIA are among the world's most inhospitable areas and many travellers exploring this region had paid with their lives. Attempts to cross the Arabian Desert were plagued with problems, including scorching heat, dehydration, and starvation. Visits to sacred sites had proved similarly difficult, as non-Muslims were forbidden to enter Islam's holy cities and anyone caught faced the death penalty. This had not deterred some explorers taking risks to gain access. Those who had survived, told their tales in books, which opened up Arabia to the Western world.

MAP KEY

- ← Route of Ludovico di Varthema (1503–05)
- ← Route of Carsten Niebuhr (1761–67)
- ← Route of Richard Burton (1851–53)
- ← Route of Harry Philby (1917–18)
- ← Route of Bertram Thomas (1930–31)
- ← Route of Harry Philby (1932)
- ← Route of Wilfred Thesiger (1946–47)
- ← Route of Wilfred Thesiger (1947–48)

▲ LAST MAN STANDING

In 1761, the King of Denmark sponsored an expedition to Arabia to collect plant and animal samples. The port of Luhayyah, shown here in ruins, was the first stop. But as the journey continued, conditions worsened. Malaria and sea travel claimed the lives of five men until only the German explorer Carsten Niebuhr was left to complete the expedition.

▼ PILGRIMAGE

For centuries, Muslims have made the pilgrimage to Mecca, Islam's holiest city, but non-believers have never been allowed inside. In 1503, the Italian explorer Ludovico di Varthema broke this rule when he became the first European non-Muslim to enter Mecca. Travelling with 40,000 pilgrims, some of whom were European converts to Islam, Varthema went undetected in the sacred city. He chronicled his controversial experience in a book published in 1510.

KA'ABA is Islam's holiest place, containing the Black Stone that is associated with Abraham

MASTER OF DISGUISE ▶

The daring British adventurer and writer Richard Burton had a deep interest in Muslim culture. He donned the disguise of a Muslim pilgrim and gained entry to the holy city in 1853. With his flair for languages, Burton could speak Arabic, so nobody who talked to him questioned his motives for being there. Burton became famous when his dangerous methods were documented in a travel book published two years after the trip to Mecca.

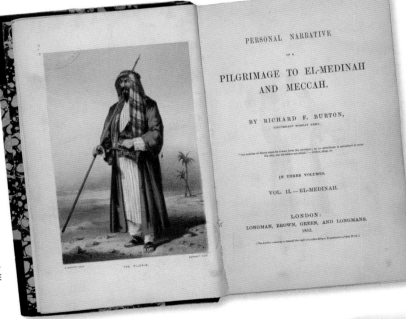

BURTON'S BOOK SHOWING A PAINTING OF HIM IN DISGUISE

DESOLATE CROSSING ▲

The Arabian Desert covers a vast area of 2,300,000 sq km (900,000 sq miles). By the 20th century, the only unexplored region was the barren Rub 'al Khali ("Empty Quarter"). In 1931, the British explorer Bertram Thomas was lucky when an unexpected shower of rain helped him pass through the dry dunes. A year later the British writer Harry Philby became the second explorer to cross the treacherous landscape on his unsuccessful mission to find the legendary city of Wabar, mentioned in Islam's holy book, the Koran.

DID YOU KNOW?

In 1905, British explorer Gertrude Bell left her comfortable life in England to travel across the Arabian Desert. The local people accepted Bell, and affectionately called her "Daughter of the Desert". She kept a record of her travels in a book called *The Desert and the Sown*, which proved popular with readers in Europe.

ROAMING THE DESERT ▶

During the 1940s, one man spent five years roaming the Rub 'al Khali region of Arabia. Celebrated British explorer Sir Wilfred Thesiger travelled with camels and lived with the local Bedouins (desert dwellers) to learn their way of life. He took thousands of photographs and recounted his experiences, including nearly dying of thirst, in his book called *Arabian Sands*.

Conquering the North Pole

NORTH AMERICA
Beaufort Sea
East Siberian Sea
ASIA
Siberia
New Siberian Islands
ARCTIC OCEAN
Laptev Sea
North Pole
Severnaya Zemlya
Ellesmere Island
Franz Josef Land
Hall Bay
Novaya Zemlya
Greenland
Svalbard
Barents Sea
Godthåb
Greenland Sea
Tromsø
Vadsø
Norwegian Sea
Iceland
EUROPE
ATLANTIC OCEAN
Leith

WHILE MOST OF THE PLANET had been explored by the 19th century, the Arctic remained a mysterious wilderness. Travelling in the frozen region was notoriously difficult because of the dangerous weather conditions and long winters of permanent darkness. At the heart of the frozen Arctic Ocean was the elusive North Pole – the northernmost point on Earth. In pursuit of glory, European and American explorers set off for the Pole. The race was finally won in 1909, although controversy still surrounds the victory today.

MAP KEY

- Voyage of Charles Hall (1871)
- First voyage of Fridtjof Nansen (1888)
- Second voyage of Fridtjof Nansen (1893–1896)
- Route of Robert Peary (1909)

▼ **COLD CLIMATE**

Arctic explorers struggled to adapt to the relentless cold. The sub-zero temperatures, drifting ice, heavy blizzards, and freezing fog made conditions hazardous and many of them turned back in defeat. Those who prevailed learned survival techniques from the native Inuit (Eskimo) people. They travelled on speedy sledges pulled by dogs and killed Arctic animals for food and clothing.

DID YOU KNOW?

American Frederick Cook claimed to have reached the North Pole in 1908, a year before Robert Peary. Their dispute was the lead story in the newspapers at that time.

◄ HALL MAKES HIS MARK

In 1860, the American newspaper publisher Charles Hall set off on the first of three expeditions to the Arctic. There, he befriended the Inuit people and became an authority on the Arctic landscape. Hall's real claim to fame was being the first person to reach northern Greenland. Just weeks after his success in 1871, Hall was found dead on board his ship *Polaris*.

ICE DRIFTER ►

History was made in 1888 when Norwegian science enthusiast Fridtjof Nansen became the first person to travel east to west across Greenland on foot. Five years later, Nansen had the ingenious idea of building a vessel that could resist ice pressure. His ship, *Fram*, froze into the ice floes and drifted along with them instead of being crushed. Though Nansen failed to get as far as the North Pole, he was hailed a hero for his ground-breaking ship design.

HOT AIR BALLOON was named *Örnen*, which means "The Eagle".

BALLOON DISASTER

wedish engineer Salomon Andrée tried a different oute to the North Pole. Taking off from the Norwegian sland of Spitsbergen in July 1897, he ascended in his ot air balloon with two companions. A storm is elieved to have brought the balloon crashing own two days later. It was not until 1930 hat the balloonists' bodies were found y Norwegian explorers.

◄ POLE POSITION

In a series of eight expeditions between 1891 and 1909, American naval commander Robert Peary travelled further and further north. On 6 April 1909, the last of his expeditions, he took this photograph of his travelling companion Matthew Henson and four Inuits, claiming they had arrived at the North Pole. Most people now accept that Peary won the race to the North Pole, though some contemporary Arctic explorers insist he could not have returned to his base in only two weeks, which he did.

HENSON at the North Pole

Race to the South Pole

THE LAST CONTINENT to be explored was the coldest, driest, and windiest place on Earth. Whale and seal hunters first set eyes on Antarctica in 1820, but it took another 70 years for scientific exploration to get underway. Explorers from all over the world made heroic attempts to cross this inhospitable land, but many of them ended up losing their lives. By the early 20th century, the hardiest adventurers had begun battling it out to reach the continent's centre – the frozen plateau of the South Pole.

MAP KEY

◄— James Clark Ross: first stage of voyage (1838–41)
◁— James Clark Ross: second stage of voyage (1841–43)
◄— Route of Ernest Shackleton (1907–09)
◄— Route of Roald Amundsen (1910–12)
◄— Route of Robert Scott (1910–12)
◄— Route of Ernest Shackleton (1914–16)

▲ A FROZEN LAND

There are no people living in Antarctica. Only cold-adapted animals such as Emperor penguins live in this frozen continent. When faced with such low temperatures and heavy blizzards, the resilient penguins can only huddle closely together. The severe conditions endured by the penguins sometimes proved fatal for explorers.

◄ NAVIGATOR NAME

The name James Clark Ross is forever linked to the Antarctic. This British naval officer discovered many remote areas of the continent, which are now named after him, such as Ross Island, Ross Ice Shelf, and Ross Sea. Much of the continent's coastline was mapped by Ross during his expedition of 1838–43.

◄ NORWAY'S WINNER

In 1910 two teams set off on the same mission – to reach the South Pole. Roald Amundsen, shown here, headed the Norwegian expedition, while Robert Scott led the British one. Amundsen triumphed on 14 December 1911, when he reached the Pole a month before Scott. Using skis and husky dogs gave Amundsen an advantage of speed.

PHOTOGRAPH OF *ENDURANCE*
TRAPPED BY PACK-ICE

CLOTHING WORN BY SCOTT
ON HIS DOOMED EXPEDITION
TO THE SOUTH POLE

▲ BRITISH TRAGEDY

Scott's team of ten explorers was gradually whittled away by inclement weather, lack of provisions, and frostbite. On 17 January 1912, five men reached the South Pole and were devastated to learn that they had lost the race. Tragically, on the return to base camp, the remaining men, including Scott, died of exhaustion and frostbite.

DID YOU KNOW?

The first person to set foot on the Antarctic Peninsula was probably the American seal hunter Captain John Davis. He claimed to have sailed to Hughes Bay in his ship *Cecilia*, and disembarked for about an hour on 7 February 1821.

◀ *ENDURANCE*

Irish explorer Ernest Shackleton dreamed of reaching the South Pole. During his first expedition of 1907, he came within 160 km (100 miles) of the Pole. In 1914, he set off in his ship *Endurance*, but his dream ended early in the waters of the Weddell Sea when dense pack-ice surrounded the vessel. Shackleton and his crew had no choice but to abandon the sinking ship. Setting up camp on icy land nearby, they could only watch as the pack-ice crushed *Endurance*. It took 11 months for the ship to disappear from view.

Ocean Exploration

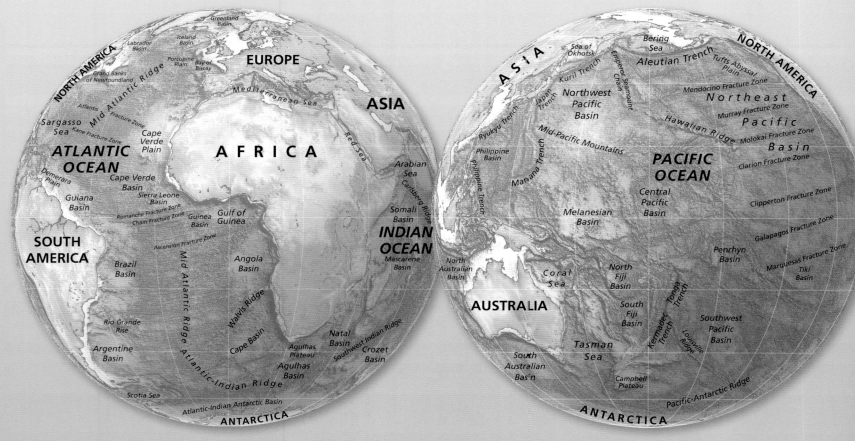

Map labels (Western hemisphere): Greenland Basin · Labrador Basin · Iceland Basin · NORTH AMERICA · EUROPE · Porcupine Plain · Bay of Biscay · Grand Banks of Newfoundland · Mid Atlantic Ridge · Mediterranean Sea · ASIA · Atlantis Fracture Zone · Kane Fracture Zone · Cape Verde Plain · ATLANTIC OCEAN · AFRICA · Red Sea · Arabian Sea · Sargasso Sea · Carlsberg Ridge · Demerara Plain · Cape Verde Basin · Sierra Leone Basin · Guinea Basin · Gulf of Guinea · Somali Basin · INDIAN OCEAN · Guiana Basin · Romanche Fracture Zone · Chain Fracture Zone · Mascarene Basin · SOUTH AMERICA · Ascension Fracture Zone · Brazil Basin · Angola Basin · Mid Atlantic Ridge · Natal Basin · Southwest Indian Ridge · Crozet Basin · Rio Grande Rise · Walvis Ridge · Cape Basin · Agulhas Plateau · Agulhas Basin · Atlantic-Indian Ridge · Argentine Basin · Scotia Sea · Atlantic-Indian Antarctic Basin · ANTARCTICA

Map labels (Eastern hemisphere): Bering Sea · NORTH AMERICA · Sea of Okhotsk · Aleutian Trench · Tufts Abyssal Plain · ASIA · Kuril Trench · Emperor Seamount Chain · Mendocino Fracture Zone · Japan Trench · Northwest Pacific Basin · Northeast · Murray Fracture Zone · Ryukyu Trench · Mid-Pacific Mountains · Hawaiian Ridge · Pacific · Molokai Fracture Zone · Philippine Basin · Basin · Clarion Fracture Zone · Mariana Trench · PACIFIC OCEAN · Philippine Trench · Central Pacific Basin · Melanesian Basin · Clipperton Fracture Zone · North Fiji Basin · Galapagos Fracture Zone · North Australian Basin · Coral Sea · Penrhyn Basin · Marquesas Fracture Zone · Tiki Basin · AUSTRALIA · South Fiji Basin · Kermadec Trench · Tonga Trench · Southwest Pacific Basin · Tasman Sea · Louisville Ridge · South Australian Bas'n · Campbell Plateau · Pacific-Antarctic Ridge · ANTARCTICA

ALTHOUGH THE OCEANS COVER TWO-THIRDS of the planet, the underwater world remained a mystery for centuries. It was not until the 1850s that studying the oceans became a science (oceanography). Explorers set off on research expeditions in preparation for the first scientific conferences held in the late 19th century. With the invention of deep-sea vehicles, diving suits, and new navigational equipment, underwater exploration was well underway by the 20th century. Mountains, ridges, deep trenches, and volcanoes were among the extraordinary features discovered on the deep ocean floor. More than half the world's oceans are now known to be deeper than 3,000 m (10,000 ft), so explorers must go to even greater depths to learn the secrets of the sea.

THESE MAPS SHOW some of the main features of the ocean floor. Just like on land, there are mountain chains, ridges, and trenches.

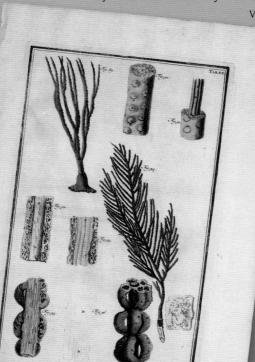

◀ MARSIGLI'S MARINE LIFE

The first underwater expedition was led by Italian count Louis Marsigli in 1706. He used fishing nets to catch samples of sea life from the Mediterranean Sea. After studying his finds under a microscope, Marsigli recorded the details in drawings such as these. His only mistake was his belief that the corals and sponges he discovered were plants, when they are really classed as animals.

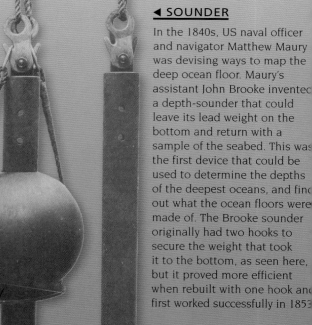

◀ SOUNDER

In the 1840s, US naval officer and navigator Matthew Maury was devising ways to map the deep ocean floor. Maury's assistant John Brooke invented a depth-sounder that could leave its lead weight on the bottom and return with a sample of the seabed. This was the first device that could be used to determine the depths of the deepest oceans, and find out what the ocean floors were made of. The Brooke sounder originally had two hooks to secure the weight that took it to the bottom, as seen here, but it proved more efficient when rebuilt with one hook and first worked successfully in 1853.

LEAD WEIGHT to assist sinking

SOUNDER WITH TWO HOOKS

SOUNDER WITH ONE HOOK

ROV HERCULES TAKING
SAMPLES FROM THE SEABED

UNDERWATER INVESTIGATORS ▲

Equipped with lights and cameras, remotely operated vehicles
(ROVs) are unmanned vehicles that can go underwater to explore
the depths, investigate shipwrecks, and carry out experiments.
As ROVs are tethered to ships on the surface, scientists on
board can use closed-circuit television to view the vehicles
and control their parts, such as the claws and sample-takers.
Though costly to run, ROVs are popular with sea scientists and
marine archaeologists because there is no risk to human life.

SCIENTIFIC VOYAGE

he first ship specially equipped for ocean exploration
as HMS *Challenger*. With two laboratories, an official
hotographer, and the latest navigational equipment,
ne ship set off in 1872 on a four-year scientific mission,
unded by the British government. Covering 110,000 km
58,000 miles) and sailing every ocean except the Arctic,
ne scientists collected samples, tested the water, and
nost importantly, showed there was marine life on
ne ocean floor.

◀ NEWT SUIT

Atmospheric diving suits (ADS), including
the newt suit shown here, allow divers
to reach depths of 1,000 m (3,280 ft),
while staying at normal atmospheric
pressure. First made in 1987, the
cast aluminium newt suit has
flexible joints, so the wearer can
perform a range of underwater
tasks, including salvage,
structural repairs, and
inspections. The main air
supply lasts eight hours,
but there is an emergency
stock if required.

NEWT SUIT DIVER WORKING
UNDERWATER ON THE
EXTERIOR OF A SUBMARINE

DID YOU KNOW?

The deepest dive ever made
was by the bathyscaphe *Trieste*
on 23 January 1960. It dived
to almost 11 km (7 miles) to
the deepest point on Earth,
called the Mariana Trench in
the Pacific Ocean.

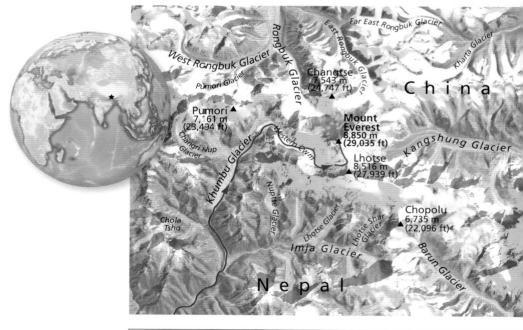

On Top of the World

MANY ANCIENT CIVILIZATIONS regarded mountains with awe. The Ancient Greeks believed their highest mountain, Olympus, was home to the gods, while South America's Incas carried out religious sacrifices on the snowcapped peaks of the Andes mountains. To travellers and traders throughout the ages, mountains were huge obstacles they had to pass. Only in the 1750s did people begin climbing mountains just to reach the top. Some ascended for scientific research, but many wanted the achievement. Despite this new interest in mountaineering, the world's highest peak, Mount Everest, was not conquered for another 200 years.

MOUNT EVEREST lies in the Himalayas – a mountain range in Asia that has the world's tallest mountains

▲ MOUNTAIN MISSIONARIES

Christian missionaries were among the first Europeans to explore the Himalayas. In 1661, two priests, called John Grueber and Albert d'Orville, set out from China before arriving in the Himalayas. They travelled over the mountains, met the locals, and descended via the Nepalese valleys, shown here.

MAP KEY

⬅ Route of Tenzing Norgay and Edmund Hillary (1953)

◀ ALPINE PIONEERS

During the 18th century, mountain climbing became very popular, as Europeans attempted to ascend the vast peaks of the Alps. The tallest mountain in this range, Mont Blanc, proved a popular challenge. Bordering both Italy and France, the mountain is 4,808 m (15,774 ft) in height and poses a great risk to climbers. Mont Blanc was finally conquered in 1786 by Italian doctor Michel-Gabriel Paccard. Switzerland's Henriette d'Angeville was the first woman to reach the top in 1838.

▲ MIGHTY EVEREST

Efforts to scale the world's highest mountain, Mount Everest on the Nepal-China border, began in the 20th century, but even with the newly invented oxygen equipment to assist the mountaineers, the climb was incredibly dangerous. Mount Everest's steep slopes and the bad weather make for a treacherous, often fatal, trip. In 1924, British climbers George Mallory and Andrew Irvine went missing when they were almost at the summit.

▲ ON MOUNT EVEREST

At least eight serious attempts were made to reach Everest's summit, before a team was successful. History was made on 29 May 1953 when Tenzing Norgay and Edmund Hillary reached the top. The sherpa guide and New Zealand's most famous mountaineer spent 15 minutes on top of the world. Since then, there have been hundreds of successful climbs.

MATTERHORN CHAMPION ▶

British artist Edward Whymper became a mountaineering legend in the 19th century. At first, he drew the stunning views of the French Alps, before making the decision to climb them. He was first to reach many of the highest peaks in this mountain range. His biggest achievement was climbing the famous Matterhorn in the Swiss Alps. Many had tried to climb it, but all had failed until Whymper reached the summit on his sixth attempt in 1865.

Race to the Moon

DURING WORLD WAR II, German scientists developed a highly powerful rocket, called the *V2*. Once the war was over, the Russians and Americans used this rocket's technology to help them build craft suitable for space travel. To escape from Earth's gravity, the craft had to fly at a staggering 28,000 kph (17,400 mph). Both nations were competing to be the first to use their own craft to land a person on the Moon. Getting astronauts safely to and from the Moon, 384,400 km (238,900 miles) away, was a monumental challenge. In 1969, the greatest achievement in the history of exploration was witnessed by many worldwide when two Americans walked on the Moon.

THIS MAP shows part of the Moon. The craters and rocky plai have been caused by space debris colliding into the Moon ove billions of years. The red dots represent the Apollo landing site

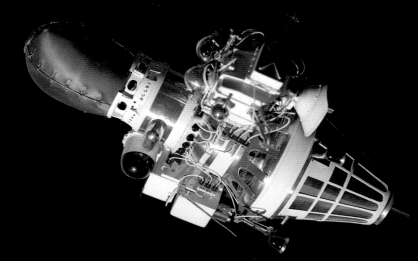

◄ FIRST LANDING

On 3 February 1966, the Russian *Luna 9* spacecraft became the first vehicle to make a soft landing on the Moon. The craft began surveying the surface and sent panoramic photographs back to Earth. This was the Russians' twelfth attempt at a soft landing and gave them a victory over the Americans. However, the craft was unmanned, so the ultimate challenge of landing a person on the Moon remained up for grabs.

APOLLO MISSIONS ►

From 1961–75, America's Apollo missions hit the headlines. As well as many unmanned expeditions, there were 11 missions with crews, including two orbiting Earth and two orbiting the Moon. History was made on 20 July 1969 when *Apollo 11*'s Neil Amstrong and Buzz Aldrin became the first people to walk on the Moon. They stayed for 2 hours, 47 minutes, and 14 seconds. Five more missions landed on the Moon over the next three years, with the astronauts taking photographs, collecting rock samples, and carrying out experiments.

APOLLO 8, seen here launching from Cape Canaveral in Florida, was the first manned mission to orbit the Moon

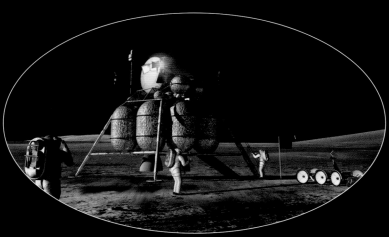

▲ PERMANENT STATION

At the American space agency NASA, plans are underway for astronauts to visit the surface of the Moon again. However, this expedition will be more than a flying visit. As shown in this artist's impression, the astronauts intend to set up stations and stay for extended periods. In the future, they hope to travel to Mars and beyond from this base.

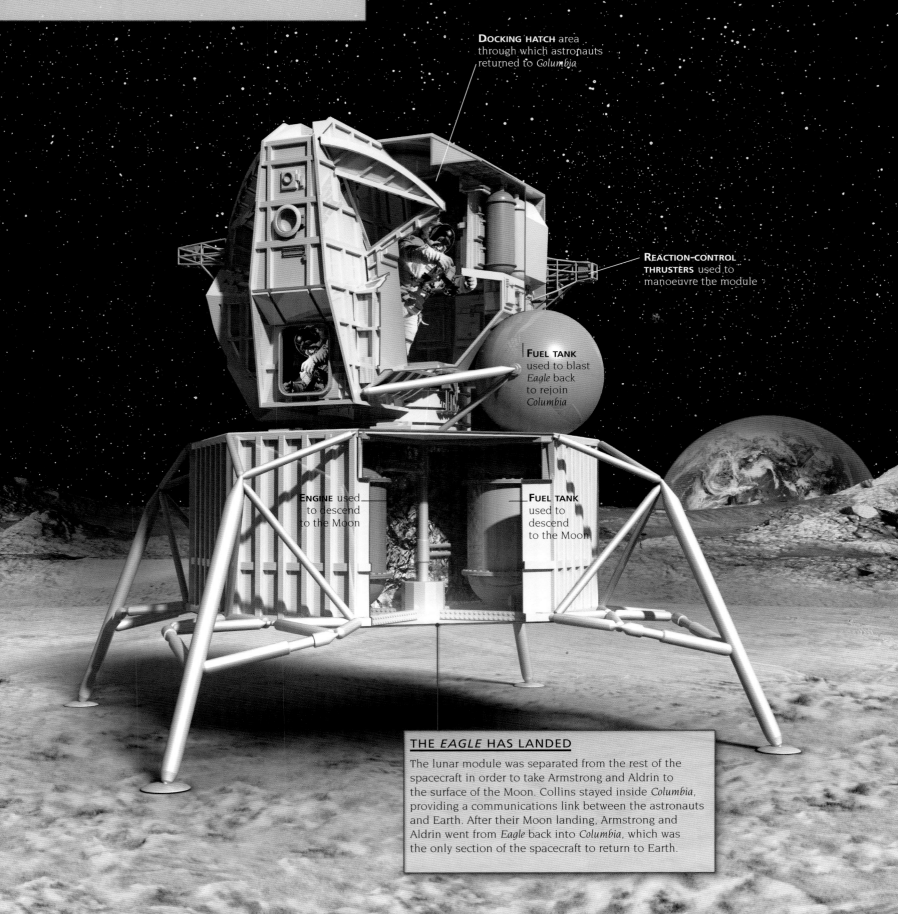

APOLLO 11

The *Apollo 11* spacecraft was made up of the lunar module, the command module, and the service module. The three astronauts Neil Armstrong, Buzz Aldrin, and Michael Collins worked and slept in the command module, called *Columbia*. The service module was attached to *Columbia* and contained all the support systems necessary for the flight. The lunar module, called *Eagle*, was the first manned vehicle to land on the Moon.

DOCKING HATCH area through which astronauts returned to *Columbia*

REACTION-CONTROL THRUSTERS used to manoeuvre the module

FUEL TANK used to blast *Eagle* back to rejoin *Columbia*

ENGINE used to descend to the Moon

FUEL TANK used to descend to the Moon

THE *EAGLE* HAS LANDED

The lunar module was separated from the rest of the spacecraft in order to take Armstrong and Aldrin to the surface of the Moon. Collins stayed inside *Columbia*, providing a communications link between the astronauts and Earth. After their Moon landing, Armstrong and Aldrin went from *Eagle* back into *Columbia*, which was the only section of the spacecraft to return to Earth.

Exploring the Planets

THE MOON LANDINGS of 1969 paved the way for further space travel, with explorers turning their attention to Earth's neighbouring planets. Ancient Greek astronomers first observed lights moving among the stars and called them planets, meaning "wanderers". These large bodies are now familiar to us, thanks to advances in robotic spacecraft. Unlike manned missions, robotic craft can conquer long distances and difficult atmospheric conditions with no risk to human life. They carry cameras and other instruments to investigate the surfaces and atmospheres of planets and their moons. Robotic craft have visited all the major planets and there are plans for human exploration of Mars.

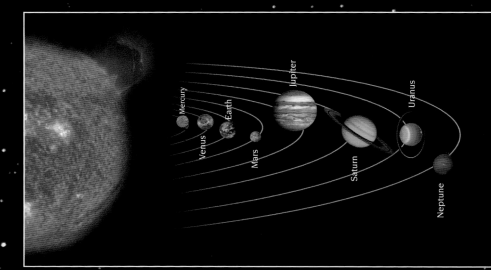

THERE ARE EIGHT PLANETS in the solar system, including Earth. Mercury is nearest the Sun, while Neptune is furthest away. Jupiter is the largest planet and Mercury is the smallest.

◀ MERCURY

NASA's spacecraft *Mariner 10* flew past the small, fast-moving planet Mercury three times in 1974 and 1975. The craft was able to map half the planet's surface and send thousands of photographs back to Earth, revealing Moon-like craters all over it. Mercury was also shown to have temperature extremes – the side facing the Sun is scorching hot, while the side furthest away is freezing cold.

▼ MARS

Named after the Roman god of war, Mars is also known as "the Red Planet". This is because of its red soil, photographed here by the NASA craft *Mars Pathfinder* in 1997. This planet most resembles Earth with its mountains, canyons, and deserts. Since the 19th century, scientists speculated that Mars may have once been home to life. No evidence was found, and soil samples taken by *Viking 1* and *2* proved inconclusive. Mars has been mapped in detail by several orbiting craft and studied by three robotic rovers, two of which (*Spirit* and *Opportunity*) are still at work.

◀ VENUS

The brightest planet is Venus, named after the Roman goddess of beauty. Russia's *Venera 3* was the first spacecraft to reach Venus in 1966, and many have visited since, with *Venera 9* taking photographs of the surface. These were the first images to be returned to Earth from the surface of another planet. The American spacecraft *Magellan* used radar technology to make maps of the surface of Venus, such as this one.

VOYAGER 1
includes telescopes,
analyzing tools,
and antennae

RED SPOT on Jupiter is a
raging storm that has been
observed from Earth for
more than 300 years

▲ VOYAGER 1

Launched from the
USA in 1977, the spacecraft
Voyager 1 travelled past Jupiter and
Saturn. When *Voyager 1* passed another
craft, *Pioneer 10*, it become the most distant
man-made object in Space. Still in operation
today, *Voyager 1* is NASA's longest lasting mission.

▲ JUPITER

Recognized by ancient civilizations, giant-sized
Jupiter could fit all the other planets inside it. Six
years after *Pioneer 10*'s fly-by, NASA's *Voyager 1* passed
Jupiter in 1979, recording active volcanoes on the
planet's moon and faint rings of dust around it.
A comet hit Jupiter in 1994, resulting in massive
fireballs. These were captured on camera by the
Hubble Space Telescope, which is permanently
stationed above Earth's atmosphere.

◀ SATURN

This giant planet is made of gas and liquid.
Although Saturn is visible to the naked
eye, the Italian astronomer Galileo was
the first person to observe it through
a telescope in the 17th century. Winds
of 1,770 kph (1,100 mph) were recorded
on Saturn by the *Voyager 1* spacecraft
in 1980. Although it looks like two
main rings circle Saturn, data collected
showed these are actually thousands
of tiny rings made up of chunks
of ice mixed with rock or dust.

INFRARED IMAGE
of Uranus shows
up clouds not visible
to the human eye

URANUS

n 13 March 1781, German astronomer William
erschel made a cosmic discovery, when he
as the first to spot the distant planet Uranus.
oyager 2 visited Uranus in 1986 and took images
f the rings encircling it. The planet appears
pped on it side, and scientists believe this is
e result of a large, celestial body colliding with
ranus in the past.

◀ NEPTUNE

The existence of Neptune was indicated when
Uranus did not follow its expected orbit
around the Sun. Calculations were worked
out, assuming that the gravity of another
planet was pulling Uranus off course,
and Neptune's position was predicted.
Named after the Roman god of the
seas, the furthest planet remained
a mystery until *Voyager 2* flew there.
Launched from the USA in 1977, the
craft took 12 years to reach Neptune.

Exploration Facts

Early explorers had no sophisticated instruments to help them find their way. Instead, they used natural signs, such as the stars and local landmarks, to help them navigate. Today, the development of high-tech instruments and maps means that more of the Earth than ever has been explored and charted. As the world becomes smaller, the nature of exploration is changing. Modern explorers face new challenges in their search to discover more about the world. The next few pages look at some of the facts about navigation, and at the work of explorers of the past and of the future.

Finding the Way

EARLY EXPLORERS had no navigational instruments to help them find their way around the world. This was particularly problematic at sea where mariners could rely only on the stars and the position of the Sun to assist their travels. Using "dead reckoning" (intelligent guesswork), sailors learned to look for signs in nature, such as wind, cloud formations, and sea currents that could influence their route. By the 15th century, however, the great age of European sea exploration was under way, and some basic instruments and maps began making voyages easier. Today, satellites, radio communication, and computers have transformed navigation. With accuracy and immediacy, explorers can find out their location, the right direction, and the remaining distance.

ASTROLABE has degrees marked out around its circular edge

POINTER

▲ COMPASS

Invented in China during the 11th century, the compass was a ground-breaking navigational tool that helped sailors find their way for centuries. Compasses work on the basis that Earth has two magnetic poles near the North and South Poles. The needle of magnetized iron will always line up with these magnetic fields, thereby pointing out the direction. It was not until 1300 that the navigator's compass we recognize today was developed in Europe.

▲ ASTROLABE

Imaginary lines called latitude circle Earth from east to west, and are measured in degrees north or south of the equator. By the Middle Ages, European sailors used a device called an astrolabe to measure the height of the Sun at noon. This enabled them to determine their latitude at sea. Navigators held astrolabes up to the Sun and where the rays shone through two holes on a pointer attached to the disc, the height of the Sun in degrees above the horizon was revealed.

◀ CHRONOMETER

Imaginary lines from north to south on Earth are called longitude. These are measured east or west of the Greenwich line in England, which co-ordinates time. In the 18th century, a very accurate clock called the chronometer was invented to calculate longitude. Mariners compared local time at noon with Greenwich time on the chronometer and used the difference to work out how many degrees east or west of Greenwich they were.

POCKET CHRONOMETER WITH ORNATE FACE AND ROMAN NUMERALS

MAPPING THE WORLD ▶

Early maps showed the world known at the time, and geographical knowledge was often limited. As a result, maps were flawed and inconsistent. The first atlas, in the form of a collection of maps and text, came from the Flemish scholar Abraham Ortelius who produced *Theatrum Orbis Terrarum* ("Theatre of the World") in 1570. Modern maps are made using satellite technology, so they are extremely accurate.

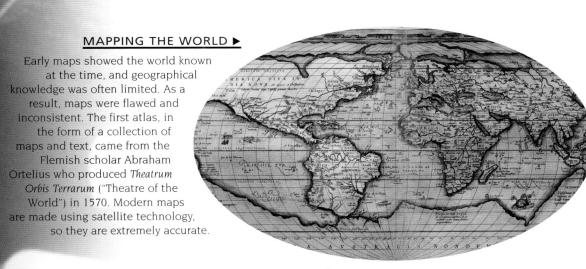

ATLAS BY ABRAHAM ORTELIUS

◀ ELECTRONIC NAVIGATION

The latest radio, radar, and satellite technology has revolutionized navigational techniques. Using handheld global positioning satellite (GPS) devices, explorers can check their exact position anywhere in the world, whether on land or at sea. These electronic devices give the user precise latitude, longitude, and altitude measurements by receiving signals via radio from satellites stationed above Earth.

SATELLITES ▶

Many satellites circle the Earth. Some are navigational satellites, which beam radio signals to Earth. Drivers and mariners use electronic equipment to pick up these signals and the information received is used to guide them. There are 24 navigational satellites in total. They stay in a fixed position 36,000 km (22,370 miles) above us, and move in orbit at the same speed as Earth.

◀ MAPPING WITH SOUND

First deployed in 1969, the US electronic mapping system *Gloria* uses reflected sound waves to produce sonographs (digital images) of the seabed. Here, *Gloria* is being loaded on to a ship. Out at sea, the ship follows a set route, while *Gloria* sends a pulse of sound to the ocean floor every 30 seconds. The echoes sent back are recorded by *Gloria* and the resulting images map the seabed with complete precision.

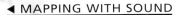

Exploring the Past

MANY SPECTACULAR ANCIENT SITES and historic treasures have been uncovered by explorers. While some locations were found by accident, many were the result of large-scale expeditions or intensive searches, and at times, great risks. Some explorers pursued glory in the race to reach these lost cities, but others sought to unearth valuables from their ruins for research purposes. Using the latest technological equipment, archaeologists are now studying these sites and treasures to learn more about the planet's past.

EGYPTIAN EXPEDITION ▶

People in Europe learned about Egypt from Napoleon Bonaparte's attempt to conquer Egypt in 1798–99. He took with him a large group of scholars. They recorded the details of the trip, including their observations at the pyramids of Giza, one of the Ancient Wonders of the World. Between 1809 and 1830, they published their findings in many volumes.

▲ LOST CITY

The ancient city of Petra in Jordan was founded in c. 300 BC and was abandoned about 400 years later when trade routes developed elsewhere. The location of this lost city was a mystery for more than a thousand years. Swiss explorer Johann Burkhardt made the breakthrough in 1812. Dressed as a Muslim pilgrim, he hired a Bedouin to take him to a holy mountain via the ruins and monuments of Petra. His trip paved the way for tourists to visit the stunning city, with its beautiful buildings.

◀ MOVING MEMNON

Italian explorer Giovanni Belzoni arrived in Egypt in 1815, searching for treasures. His achievements included investigating the temples of Edfu and Karnak, clearing temple of Abu Simbel of sand, and ente the second pyramid at Giza. At the requ of the British consul, Belzoni transported the huge bust of Young Memnon (Pharac Rameses II) to England to be displayed.

ANGKOR WAT ▶

Although other Europeans had visited the temple of Angkor Wat in Cambodia, it was French explorer Henry Mouhot's trip in 1861 that captured the public imagination. Thanks to Mouhot's in-depth reports and detailed drawings, the temple and city of Angkor became popular in the West. Today, the home of the ancient Khmer civilization is Cambodia's biggest tourist attraction.

▲ CAVE COLLECTION

Hungarian-born archaeologist Aurel Stein collected many treasures from his journeys around Central Asia. Today, these objects are on display in museums all over the world. His greatest find was the 1907 discovery of the Mogoa Caves, known as the Caves of the Thousand Buddhas, in Dunhuang, China. The caves contained ornate sculptures, paintings, and textiles, as well as thousands of ancient Buddhist scriptures.

NCA TRAIL

911, the American archaeologist Hiram Bingham nd the ancient Inca city of Machu Picchu in the uvian Andes. This exciting discovery led Bingham front many more expeditions to other parts of South erica. Machu Picchu is now one of the continent's st popular tourist attractions. Every year, thousands people follow the Inca trail past the ruins of old vns, such as Ollantayumbe, shown above, and to the stunning site, high in the mountains.

◄ ANCIENT ARTWORK

Archaeologists have learned about ancient peoples by exploring caves. The dark, cool conditions of caves can preserve their contents for thousands of years. In 1985, for example, Henri Cosquer found a cave at Cape Morgiou in France. Paintings and engravings were discovered on the walls. Now named Cosquer Cave, the pictures include animals, hands, and geometric symbols. These works have been dated at more than 20,000 years old.

BUILDING is designed to resemble Mount Meru, home of the Hindu gods

Exploring the Future

IN THE 21ST CENTURY, much of the world has been explored. Every continent has been reached, and some of the most inhospitable and remote locations are now familiar to us. Far-flung places are accessible to all, with tourists visiting the North and South Poles, and even travelling into space. Today, the explorers are scientists and conservationists. Their studies and projects hold the key to understanding the fragile planet. These modern explorers are learning about changing habitats, climates, and threats in the hope of preserving Earth for many future generations.

RICE FIELDS in Ghandrung, Nepal, are terraced so water cannot run downhill and crops stay moist

LOST RAINFORESTS ▶

With rainforests disappearing rapidly, scientists are studying these habitats to find better ways of managing them. Their research has led to new species of animals, birds, and plants being found as well as attempts to preserve known species. At this rehabilitation centre in Indonesia, people take care of orphaned orangutans until they can be returned safely to the wild.

▼ FUTURE FARMING

In some parts of the world, farming is under threat. Where loggers have felled trees, wind and rain have worn away soil (soil erosion). There are catastrophic mud slides and farmers face an uncertain future. Conservation projects are monitoring these problems, particularly in mountainous regions, such as the Middle Hills area of Nepal. The Middle Hills project is working to restore lost forests by planting trees and protecting these new plantations. Local communities have chosen trees and plants that will provide a range of produce.

SCIENTIST studying the desert dunes of Oman

DESERTIFICATION

Some of the world's deserts are expanding, and this process is called desertification. Excessive logging and continual farming of land have worn out the soil and caused the problem to spread. Projects such as the Wahiba Sands Project in Oman aim to investigate the sands and find out how to reduce the spread of deserts.

▼ REMOTE RESEARCH

The only settlements on the remote continent of Antarctica are scientific stations. The unique landscape is so special for scientists that 24 countries have already set up bases here, studying the climate and wildlife, as well as the impact of global warming on the ice. Facilities on site include laboratories, workshops, dormitories, and kitchens. The American base McMurdo is the largest station, with room for 1,000 scientists and support staff.

◄ SPACE TRAVEL

Space exploration only became a reality in 1957 when the Russians launched the first space satellite, *Sputnik I.* Now the Moon has been visited and there are plans for a manned landing on Mars. Customers can also pay to travel by spacecraft and look back at Earth. The limitless expanse of space, however, remains unknown and is still one of the biggest challenges for explorers.

WEATHER BALLOON BOX contains instruments to measure atmospheric pressure and temperature

BENEATH THE ICE ▶

Scientific research into what lies beneath the Polar ice caps is now possible thanks to remotely operated vehicles (ROVs). Designed to operate under ice and at great depths, ROVs record their findings for sea scientists to study. Intrepid divers also swim through holes in the ice to explore the seabed and view the unique life forms.

Glossary

ALPINE

A term referring to the mountain range of the Alps in Europe.

ALTITUDE

The height of a place on land measured from sea level.

AMPHORA

A two-handled pottery jar used for storing wine, oil, and other goods.

ANTARCTIC CIRCLE

An imaginary line of latitude in the Southern Hemisphere south of which there is at least one day of 24-hour sunshine and at least one day of 24-hour darkness per year.

ARCHAEOLOGIST

A person who studies the past by the scientific excavation and analysis of ancient remains.

ARCHIPELAGO

A group, or chain, of islands.

ARCTIC CIRCLE

An imaginary line of latitude in the Northern Hemisphere north of which there is at least one day of 24-hour sunshine and at least one day of 24-hour darkness per year.

ASTROLABE

An instrument used by early navigators to determine the height of the Sun and so work out their location.

ATMOSPHERIC DIVING SUIT (ADS)

A diving suit with articulated joints in the arms and legs, and an in-built air supply.

BACKSTAFF

A navigational instrument used to measure the height of the Sun or the Moon.

BOTANIST

A person who collects plants and studies their classification and structure.

CANAANITES

The ancestors of the Phoenicians who came from Canaan (an area that now covers Lebanon stretching south to the borders of Sinai).

CAPE

An area of land that juts out into a sea.

CARAVAN

A group of traders and other travellers making a journey together, often by camel or on horseback.

CARAVEL

A two- or three-masted trading ship developed by Europeans in the 15th century.

CHRONOMETER

A reliably accurate portable clock that was invented for use at sea in order to determine longitude.

CIVILIZATIONS

Human societies that have reached a high level of social, political, artistic, and economic achievement.

CODEX

A manuscript folded into a book that was used in Europe and the Americas. Plural: Codices.

COLONIES

Settlements made by people who have left their homeland in search of new places to live, but still maintain their links with their homeland. These people are known as colonists.

COMPASS

A navigational instrument, used for finding direction. A compass has a magnetized needle, which points to magnetic north.

CONQUISTADOR

A Spanish conqueror of South America.

CONSERVATIONIST

A person who helps to protect the natural world and its resources – plants, wildlife, and their habitats – for the future.

CONTINENT

A huge area of land. There are seven continents on Earth: Asia, Australasia, Africa, Europe, North America, South America, and Antarctica.

DHOW

A traditional Arab sailing ship with one or more triangular sails.

EBONY

The heavy, hard, dark wood that comes from a species of tree.

EMPIRE

A state and the lands and people that it has conquered.

EQUATOR

An imaginary circular line around the Earth – midway between the North and South Poles.

EVOLUTION

The gradual change in the characteristics of animals or plants over many generations.

FRANKINCENSE

A sweet-smelling gum that comes from trees growing in Africa and Arabia.

GEOLOGIST

A scientist who studies the origin, structure, and composition of the Earth.

GLOBAL POSITIONING SYSTEM (GPS)

A navigation system that uses signals from satellites in space to determine location.

HITTITES

A people from Anatolia (modern Turkey) c. 2000–1000 BC who built up a great empire stretching into what is now Syria.

ICEBREAKER

A ship with a strong hull and powerful engines that enable it to sail through sea-ice.

INCENSE

Fragrant herbs or spices that are burned to give off a sweet smell.

INUIT

The groups of people who live in the Arctic regions of Alaska, Greenland, and Canada. Their lives, culture, and mythology are closely linked to the harsh landscape they live in.

KA'BAH

A cube-shaped building located inside the Great Mosque in Mecca. It is the holiest place in Islam.

KNORR

A wide-bodied ship used by the Vikings for trading. It was built of oak and pine wood. It had one mast with a square sail and steering oars.

:H
...all, two-masted wooden sailing
... specially designed for use in icy
...ic waters.

...TUDE
...maginary line around the globe that
...ks how far to the north or south of the
...ator a place is.

...GITUDE
...maginary line around the globe that
...ks how far to the east or west you are
...n a fixed point.

...AR
...thing connected with the Moon.

...ORI
...e group of Polynesians and the first
...abitants of New Zealand.

...CCA
...ty in modern Saudi Arabia that is the
...hplace of the Prophet Muhammad.
... Islam's holiest city.

...GRATING
...ds and other animals that are making
...ng journey between their feeding and
...eding grounds. Also refers to people
...o move from one country to another.

...NOANS
... name given to the people who lived on
... island of Crete from about 2000–1450 BC.

...SSIONARY
...eligious person who travels to different
...ts of the world in order to convert others
...his or her faith.

...NGOLS
...omadic and war-like people from Mongolia
...o conquered a vast empire in the 1200s
...der the leadership of Genghis Khan.

...NSOON
...easonal pattern of wind that affects the
...ather, especially in southern Asia.

...USLIMS
...ople who follow the religion of Islam,
...ich began in Arabia (modern Saudi Arabia)
...D 622.

MUTINY
A revolt against authority. For example, sailors and soldiers who rebel against their officers.

MYCENAEANS
A people who dominated mainland Greece from about 1600–1100 BC.

MYRRH
A resin from trees found growing in Africa and Arabia, used as incense and in medicines.

NATURALISTS
Scientists, such as biologists, zoologists, botanists, and ecologists, who study the natural world.

NAVIGATOR
A person who plots the path or position of a ship or other vehicle. The term was also used to describe a person who explored by ship.

NEW WORLD
The term used for the Americas after their discovery in the 16th century by European explorers.

OLD WORLD
The term used to describe Africa, Europe, and Asia after the discovery of the Americas.

ORBIT
To move in a circular path around the Earth.

PAPYRUS
A tall, reed-like plant that grows in swamps in northern Africa and southern Europe. In ancient times, papyrus stems were used by the Egyptians to make paper.

PENINSULA
A narrow strip of land that is surrounded by water on three of its sides.

PHOENICIANS
Name given to the people who lived in cities along the eastern Mediterranean coast from about 1100 BC.

PILGRIM
A person who undertakes a journey to places that are sacred to their religion or beliefs.

PLANET
A large, spherical mass in space that orbits a star.

POLE
The most northerly and southerly points on Earth.

POLE STAR
The brightest star in the constellation of Ursa Minor, which is situated above the celestial North Pole.

POLYNESIANS
People whose ancestors left southeast Asia from about 2000 BC onwards and sailed to the Pacific islands.

RAPIDS
Part of a river where the water flows very fast and is very turbulent.

REMOTELY OPERATED VEHICLE (ROV)
A vehicle that is used for deep-sea exploration. ROVs are equipped with instruments and are tethered to a control ship.

SATELLITE
An artificial device that orbits the Earth and transmits information, which can be used for purposes such as navigation and mapping.

SOLAR SYSTEM
The whole family of objects that orbit the Sun.

SONAR
A system that uses pulses of sound waves to detect the presence of solid objects.

SOUNDER
An instrument used for measuring the depth of water by using a weight at the end of a rope.

SPACE
The vast, mostly empty, region in which the Sun, Earth, and all stars exist.

STRAIT
A narrow channel of sea between two areas of land.

SUBMERSIBLE
A vehicle like a mini-submarine that is built for diving to great depths in the ocean.

SUMMIT
The highest point of a mountain.

Index

Credits

The publisher would like to thank the following for their kind permission to reproduce their photographs:
Abbreviations key: a-above, b-below/bottom, c-centre, f-far, l-left, r-right, t-top

360 Degree History Research Group/Selva Egeli: 8-9; 4Corners Images: SIME/Roberto Rinaldi 38cla, 46b, 55t; akg-images: 9cr, 24bl, 27bl, 29br, 29crb, 46cl, 48bl; Academia de San Fernando, Madrid 42br; Archiv fur Kunst & Geschichte 51tl, 56crb, 69tr; Bibliotheque Nationale 21cr; Hervé Champollion 6l; Erich Lessing 7br, 7t, 9tl, 14tr, 16c, 26bl; Musee Paul Dupuy, Toulouse 88tr; Juergen Sorges 4tl, 16-17; Staatliche Schloesser und Gaerten, Berlin 64c; Alamy Images: Bill Bachman 71t; Tibor Bognar 28-29; Bruce Coleman Inc. 11cr; Deco Images 38cb, 45tl; Kevin Foy 34l; Simon Grosset 56b, 60-61; David Hancock 71br; Doug Houghton 49cb; Roy Hsu 91tl; imagebroker 22-23; Images of Africa Photobank 24tl, 30-31; Ian Arnold Images 90-91b; Craig Lovell 40bl; Mary Evans Picture Library 53br; Angus McComiskey 18c; Phil McDermott 92b; North Wind Picture Archives 41tr, 47bl, 49ca, 63c, 63tl; Beren Patterson 45br; Photo Network 84-85; Pictorial Press Ltd 69cr; The Print Collector 68bc; Richard Wareham Fotografie 13t; Robert Harding Picture Library Ltd 61cr, 75tr; Helene Rogers 73t; Royal Geographical Society 56tl, 81br, 93tl; StockShot 89cr; Joan Swinnerton 28cr; Sylvia Cordaiy Photo Library Ltd 38clb, 41l; Ariadne Van Zandbergen 31r; View Stock 4cra, 20tl; Visual Arts Library, London 54b, 63tc; David Wall 27br, 34-35; World History Archive 18tl; Ancient Art & Architecture Collection: C. Hellie 9br; R. Sheridan 27bc; Uniphoto 31b, 32cr; Art Directors & TRIP: Helene Rogers 17tr; The Art Archive: 24cb, 29tr, 67bl, 90c; British Library 30cl, 61tl; British Museum/Harper Collins Publishers 52bc; Marc Charmet/ Bibliothèque Mazarine, Paris 4ca, 19c; Dagli Orti (A)/National Museum Karachi 7c; Dagli Orti (A)/San Vitale Ravenna Italy 19tl; Dagli Orti/Museu do Caramulo, Portugal 35c; Dagli Orti/National Archaeological Museum Athens 7bl; Museo del Oro Bogota 47br; Bibliothèque Nationale, Paris 27tr; Alfredo Dagli Orti 89tr; Gianni Dagli Orti/Biblioteca Nazionale Marciana Venice 45tr; Gianni Dagli Orti/General Archive of the Indies Seville 40br; Gianni Dagli Orti/Musée des Arts Africains et Océaniens 66b; Gianni Dagli Orti/Musée du Château de Versailles 45bl; Gianni Dagli Orti/Museo de la Torre del Oro Seville 36c; Tate Gallery London 53bl; The Bridgeman Art Library: Boltin Picture Library 42bl; Bristol City Museum and Art Gallery, UK 36tr; Mitchell Library, State Library of New South Wales 70br; National Library of Australia, Canberra 71c; Nationalmuseum, Stockholm, Sweden 51tr; Private Collection/Roger Perrin 21cl; Royal Geographical Society, London, UK 67tl, 68bl; Scott Polar Research Institute, Cambridge, UK 77tr; The Stapleton Collection 56cla, 73c; The Trustees of the British Museum: 11tr, 17tc; Bryan and Cherry Alexander Photography: 59cl, 74b; Camera Press: Gamma/Patrick Aventurier 92t; Christov Effects and Design, Inc./Lubo Hristov: 12b; Corbis: Paul Almasy 17tl; Tom Bean 48r; Bettmann 63tr, 75tl, 77; Pierre Colombel 91tr; Patrick Durand 13r; Owen Franken 14bl; Peter Guttman 38ca, 51c; Hulton Archive 76br; Jacques Langevin 58t; Georgia Lowell 62t; Charles O'Rear 34cr; Philadelphia Museum of Art 33r; PoodlesRock 49cr; Jose Fuste Raga 90tr; Sergei Remezov 93cl; Stapleton Collection 81bl; Staffan Widstrand 56clb, 64-65b; DK Images: Rowan Greenwood 86-87 (background); Eye Ubiquitous: Hutchison Picture Library/Jesco von Puttkamer 47t; FLPA: Foto Natura/Rinie van Muers 50-51; Frans Lanting 59tl; Minden Pictures 49br, 76bl; Fritz Polking 56cra, 76c; Getty Images: AFP/Behrouz Mehri 72b; AFP/Goh Chai Hin 24cla, 33l; Hulton Archive 75br; LL/Roger Viollet 81cr; National Geographic/Mark Cosslett 80bl; Photographer's Choice/Alvis Upitis 61br; Dan Rafla 80-81; Heidelberg University Library: 13clb; Hemispheres Images: Bruno Barbier 10-11; Jean du Boisberranger 13bl; Franck Guiziou 18-19, 21t, 26-27; Michael Holford: 4clb, 6b; Courtesy of Lockheed Martin Aeronautics Company, Palmdale: 89br; Mary Evans Picture Library: 50c, 75bl; Pascal Meunier: 72tr; NASA: 82br; John Frassanito and Associates 82bl; JPL 84b, 84cr, 84tl, 84tr, 85bl, 85br, 85tl; The Natural History Museum, London: 65br, 65cl, 65tl, 65tr, 79cr; naturepl.com: John Downer 68-69; Warwick Sloss 14r; Staffan Widstrand 52-53; NOAA: 78br, 79t, 93bl; PA Photos: Jean Clottes 91c; Photolibrary: Hawaiian Legacy Archive 10tl; Photoshot / NHPA: A.N.T. Photol Library 70l; Martin Harvey 19tr; Dave Watts 40cl; Pitt Rivers Museum, University of Oxford: Wilfred Thesiger (2004_130_12990) 73b; RIA Novosti: 59b, 82tl; Robert Harding Picture Library: John Henry Claude Wilson 31c; Science Photo Library: British Antarctic Survey 93r; NERC/Institute of Oceanographic Sciences 89l; Alexis Rosenfeld 79b; Still Pictures: Ariadne Van Zandbergen 67; SuperStock: 62br, 66tr; age fotostock 63b, 64tl; David Towersey: 22tl, 50bl; Werner Forman Archive: Thjodminjasafn, Reykjavik, Iceland (National Museum) 23tl

Jacket images: Front: Alamy Images: ImageState fbl; Corbis: PoodlesRock fcrb; Mary Evans Picture Library: fbr; NASA: fclb; National Geographic Image Collection: Richard Nowitz t. Back: Alamy Images: ImageState fbl; Corbis: PoodlesRock fcrb; Getty Images: The Image Bank/Macduff Everton t; Mary Evans Picture Library: br; NASA: fclb. Spine: Alamy Images: Ali Kabas

All other images © Dorling Kindersley
For further information see: www.dkimages.com
The publisher would also like to thank Simon Adams, and Lynn Bresler for the index.